THE LITTLE BLACK BOOK OF

POLITICAL
WISDOM

ALSO IN THIS SERIES:

THE LITTLE BLACK BOOK OF

POLITICAL WISDOM

Edited by Sanford L. Jacobs

Skyhorse Publishing

Skyhorse Publishing books may be purchased in bulk at special discounts for sales promotion, corporate gifts, fund-raising, or educational purposes. Special editions can also be created to specifications. For details, contact the Special Sales Department, Skyhorse Publishing, 307 West 36th Street, 11th Floor, New York, NY 10018 or info@skyhorsepublishing.com.

Skyhorse® and Skyhorse Publishing® are registered trademarks of Skyhorse Publishing, Inc.®, a Delaware corporation.

Visit our website at www.skyhorsepublishing.com.

10 9 8 7 6 5 4 3 2 1

Library of Congress Cataloging-in-Publication Data is available on file.

Cover design by Danielle Ceccolini

Images courtesy of Thinkstock

ISBN: 978–1–62914–436–8
Ebook ISBN: 978–1–63220–029–7

Printed in China

Contents

Introduction

In this book you will find quotations by politicians, philosophers, economists, tycoons, journalists, comedians, judges, poets, novelists, historians, and many others, including the dictatorial Mao Zedong, the naughty Mae West, and the humble Pope Francis. As the title promises, a goodly amount of political wisdom is sprinkled across these pages. A profound example is from Plato's *Republic*, written more than 2,500 years ago: "Mankind will never see an end of trouble until lovers of wisdom come to hold political power, or the holders of power become lovers of wisdom."

That's what contemporary Turkish-born writer Mehmet Murat ildan meant when he wrote: "A very wise quote is a spectacular waterfall! When you see it, you feel its power." One of my favorites was written by the highly regarded Portuguese novelist José Maria de Eça de Queiroz, who died in 1900: "Politicians and diapers should be changed frequently, and all for the same reason."

The Internet makes it easy to find quotations; I got the text of Pope Francis's November 2013 Papal Exhortation from the

Vatican's website, vatican.va, in less than a minute. Some presidential libraries and universities allow online access to their digitized collections of official documents, speeches, and other public papers of former presidents. Senate.gov is a great source of senatorial lore and history. For some reason the House of Representatives lacks a similar digital resource.

But anyone using quotations from the web should be wary. With some exceptions, such as wikiquote.org and goodreads.com, a lot of websites include quotations with erroneous attributions. Here's a blatant example (I'd like to believe it was posted to fool the clueless and amuse those who know history): "The problem with quotes on the Internet is you never know if they are genuine."—Joseph Stalin (1879–1953).

Twitter, Facebook, and YouTube all receive endless volumes of political palaver and videos from politicians, pundits, bloggers, and other digitally enabled political junkies. Of the few social media items I kept for the book, this is one of my favorites: "If Babies Had Guns, They Wouldn't Be Aborted." That's an April 2013 tweet from Congressman Steve Stockman, a Texas Tea Party Republican. His non sequitur quickly went viral; a Google search a year later turned up a million results.

An appropriate quotation to end my introduction to *The Little Black Book of Political Wisdom* is taken from Alexander Hamilton's speech to the Constitutional Convention of 1787: "There can be no truer principle than this—that every individual of the community at large has an equal right to the protection of the government."

Amen. Buy the book. It'll help the economy.

Sanford L. Jacobs

Chapter 1

Politics and Politicians

One of the penalties for refusing to participate in politics is that you end up being governed by your inferiors.

—PLATO, *The Republic* (c. 380 BC)

• • •

Politics, as a practice, whatever its professions, has always been the systematic organization of hatreds.

—HENRY ADAMS, *The Education of Henry Adams* (1907)

• • •

What then is the American, this new man? He is either an European, or the descendant of the European, hence that strange mixture of blood, which you will find in no other country.... Here individuals of all nations are melted into a new race of men, whose labors and posterity will one day cause great changes in the world.

—JOHN HECTOR ST. JOHN, *Letters from an American Farmer* (1782)

• • •

The whole aim of practical politics is to keep the populace alarmed (and hence clamorous to be led to safety) by menacing it with an endless series of hobgoblins, all of them imaginary.

—H. L. MENCKEN

• • •

Politics are almost as exciting as war, and quite as dangerous. In war you can be killed once, but in politics many times.

—WINSTON CHURCHILL

• • •

That's one of my Goddamn precious American rights,
not to think about politics.
—JOHN UPDIKE, *Rabbit Redux* (1971)

• • •

Politics has got so expensive that it takes lots of
money to even get beat with.
—WILL ROGERS

• • •

What is the first part of politics? Education. The second?
Education. And the third? Education.
—JULES MICHELET

• • •

Finality is not the language of politics.
—BENJAMIN DISRAELI

• • •

I agree with you that in politics the middle way is none at all.
—JOHN ADAMS

• • •

In politics, what begins in fear usually ends in folly.
—SAMUEL TAYLOR COLERIDGE

• • •

In politics, there is no use looking beyond the next fortnight.
—NEVILLE CHAMBERLAIN

• • •

Politics is the art of turning influence into affluence.
—PHILANDER CHASE JOHNSON, *Senator Sorghum's Primer of Politics* (1906)

• • •

They politics like ours profess, the greater prey upon the less.
—MATTHEW GREEN, *The Grotto* (1732)

• • •

If American politics are too dirty for women to take part in, there's something wrong with American politics.
—EDNA FERBER

• • •

Politicians are the same all over. They promise to build a bridge even where there is no river.
—NIKITA KHRUSHCHEV

• • •

Without alienation, there can be no politics.
—ARTHUR MILLER

• • •

In politics, stupidity is not a handicap.
—NAPOLEON BONAPARTE

• • •

Politicks are now nothing more than means of rising in the world. With this sole view do men engage in politicks, and their whole conduct proceeds upon it.
—JAMES BOSWELL, *Life of Samuel Johnson* (1791)

• • •

Just because you do not take an interest in politics, doesn't mean politics won't take an interest in you.
—PERICLES (attributed)

• • •

Therefore, the good of man must be the objective
of the science of politics.
—ARISTOTLE, *Nicomachean
Ethics* (353 BC)

• • •

You have all the characteristics of a popular politician: a
horrible voice, bad breeding and a vulgar manner.
—ARISTOPHANES, *The Knights* (c. 424 BC)

• • •

There is little place in the political scheme of things for an
independent, creative personality, for a fighter. Anyone who
takes that role must pay a price.
—SHIRLEY CHISHOLM

• • •

Politicians are people who, when they see light at the end of
the tunnel, go out and buy some more tunnel.
—SIR JOHN QUINTON

• • •

Being in politics is like being a football coach. You have to be smart enough to understand the game and dumb enough to think it's important.

—EUGENE MCCARTHY

• • •

I have learned that one of the most important rules of politics is poise—which means looking like an owl after behaving like a jackass.

—RONALD REAGAN

• • •

Whenever a man has cast a longing eye on [offices] a rottenness begins in his conduct.

—THOMAS JEFFERSON

• • •

All politicians should have three hats—one to throw into the ring, one to talk through, and one to pull rabbits out of if elected.

—CARL SANDBURG

• • •

a politician is an arse upon which everyone
has sat except a man.
—E. E. CUMMINGS

• • •

Every politician should have been born an orphan
and remain a bachelor.
—LADY BIRD JOHNSON

• • •

Politicians and diapers should be changed frequently
and all for the same reason.
—JOSÉ MARIA DE EÇA DE QUEIROZ

• • •

We hang the petty thieves and appoint the
great ones to public office.
—AESOP

• • •

All of us who are concerned for peace and triumph of reason
and justice must be keenly aware how small an influence
reason and honest good will exert upon events
in the political field.
—ALBERT EINSTEIN

• • •

Government

[I]t's time to call in the physicists, the people who study black holes and death stars. That's what the federal government looks like after expanding ever outward for the past 224 years.
—DANIEL HENNINGER

• • •

To form a new government requires infinite care and unbounded attention; for if the foundation is badly laid, the superstructure must be bad.
—GEORGE WASHINGTON

• • •

The legitimate powers of the government extend to such acts only as are injurious to others. It does me no injury for my neighbor to say there are twenty gods or no god. It neither picks my pocket nor breaks my leg.
—THOMAS JEFFERSON, *Notes on the State of Virginia* (1785)

• • •

Does thou not know, my son, with how little wisdom the world is governed?
—COUNT AXEL OXENSTIERNA

• • •

It is important to remember there still exist other forms of government in the world today, and that dozens of foreign countries still long for a democracy such as ours to be imposed on them.

—JON STEWART

• • •

He who exercises government by means of his virtue may be compared to the North Polar Star, which keeps its place and all the stars turn towards it.

—CONFUCIUS, *The Analects of Confucius*

• • •

In the government of the sage,
He keeps their hearts vacuous,
Fills their bellies,
Weakens their ambitions,
And strengthens their bones,
He always causes his people to be without cunning or desire,
And the craft to be afraid to act.

—LAO-TZU

• • •

On my arrival in the United States, I was struck
by the degree of ability among the governed and
the lack of it among the governing.
—ALEXIS DE TOCQUEVILLE,
Democracy in America (1835)

• • •

Every dictator uses religion as a prop to
keep himself in power.
—BENAZIR BHUTTO

• • •

If we can but prevent the government from wasting the
labours of the people, under the pretence of taking care of
them, they must become happy.
—THOMAS JEFFERSON

• • •

Unluckily, governments cannot be enlightened, and a
government which regards itself a diffuser of light is the least
open to enlightenment.
—HONORÉ DE BALZAC

• • •

We, the people, recognize that this government belongs to us
. . . we can't just sit on the sidelines.
—BARACK OBAMA

• • •

The object of government in peace and in war is not the glory
of rulers or of races, but the happiness of the common man.
—WILLIAM HENRY BEVERIDGE, *Social Insurance
and Allied Services* (1942)

• • •

A government that is big enough to give you all you want is
big enough to take it all away.
—BARRY GOLDWATER

• • •

Only in time of fear is government thrown back to its
primitive and sole function of self-defense and the many
interests of which it is the guardian become
subordinated to that.
—JANE ADDAMS

• • •

When the people fear the government there is tyranny, when the government fears the people there is liberty.
—THOMAS JEFFERSON

• • •

Today, our heads are in the lion's mouth, and we must get them out the best way we can. To contend against the government is as difficult as it is to sit in Rome and fight with the Pope.
—JOHN ROCK

• • •

To change the government at this point is neither possible nor desirable. All that is necessary to be done is to make the government consistent with itself, and render the rights of the states compatible with sacred rights on human nature.
—FREDERICK DOUGLASS

• • •

There can be no truer principle than this—that every individual of the community at large has an equal right to the protection of the government.
—ALEXANDER HAMILTON

• • •

Giving money and power to government is like giving
whiskey and car keys to teenage boys.
—P. J. O'ROURKE, *Parliament of Whores* (1991)

• • •

A society of sheep must in time beget a government of wolves.
—BERTRAND DE JOUVENEL

• • •

The government solution to any problem is usually
at least as bad as the problem.
—MILTON FRIEDMAN

• • •

When any of the four pillars of government—religion, justice,
counsel, and treasure—are mainly shaken or weakened, men
had need to pray for fair weather.
—SIR FRANCIS BACON

• • •

The supply of government exceeds the demand.
—LEWIS H. LAPHAM

• • •

Democracy is two wolves and a lamb voting on what to have
for lunch. Liberty is a well-armed lamb contesting the vote!
—BENJAMIN FRANKLIN

• • •

Democracy, which means despair of finding
any heroes to govern you.
—THOMAS CARLYLE (attributed)

• • •

For the moment, therefore, democracy has won its global
near-monopoly as basis for legitimate rule in a setting which
largely contradicts its own pretensions.
—JOHN DUNN

• • •

Democracy is a charming form of government, full of variety
and disorder, and dispensing a sort of equality to
equals and unequal alike.
—PLATO, *THE REPUBLIC*

• • •

Democracy means government by the uneducated, while aristocracy means government by the badly educated.
—G. K. CHESTERTON

• • •

The strongest democracies flourish from frequent and lively debate, but they endure when people of every background and belief find a way to set aside smaller differences in the service of a greater purpose.
—BARACK OBAMA

• • •

It's not the voting that's democracy; it's the counting.
—TOM STOPPARD, *Jumpers* (1972)

• • •

Democracy's a very fragile thing. You have to take care of democracy. As soon as you stop being responsible to it and allow it to turn into scare tactics, it's no longer democracy, is it? It's something else. It may be an inch away from totalitarianism.
—SAM SHEPARD

• • •

The end of democracy and the defeat of the American Revolution will occur when government falls into the hands of the lending institutions and moneyed incorporations.
—THOMAS JEFFERSON

• • •

Wise politicians will be cautious about fettering the government with restrictions that cannot be observed, because they know that every break of the fundamental laws, though dictated by necessity, impairs that sacred reverence which ought to be maintained in the breast of rulers towards the constitution of a country.
—ALEXANDER HAMILTON

• • •

When government disappears, it's not as if paradise will take its place. When governments are gone, other interests will take their place.
—LAWRENCE LESSIG

• • •

When threatened the first thing a democracy
gives up is democracy.
—MIGNON McLAUGHLIN, *The Complete Neurotic's
Notebook* (1981)

• • •

A democracy cannot long endure with the head of
a God and the tail of a demon.
—ALEXANDER CRUMMELL

• • •

Strip American democracy and religions of its verbiage
and you find the Neanderthal.
—J. A. ROGERS

• • •

Chapter 2

Elections

Popularity should be no scale for the election of politicians. If it would depend on popularity, Donald Duck and the Muppets would take seats in the Senate.
—ORSON WELLES

• • •

The hardest thing about any political campaign is how to win without proving that you are unworthy of winning.
—ADLAI E. STEVENSON II

• • •

My favorite political philosopher is Mike Tyson. Mike Tyson once said everyone has a plan until you punch them in the face. Then they don't have a plan anymore. [The Republicans] may have a plan to beat my guy. My job is to punch them in the face.
—JIM MESSINA

• • •

After an election cycle in which an estimated $6 billion was spent on races for the presidency and Congress, the American voters—who by every account are disgusted with Washington and desperately want change—vote to keep everything pretty much the same.
—DAVE BARRY

• • •

Every election is a sort of advance auction sale of stolen goods.
—H. L. MENCKEN

• • •

People never lie so much as after a hunt, during a war or before an election.
—OTTO VON BISMARCK

• • •

The professional politician, with his eye on the next election, quite naturally seeks to temporize or completely avoid potentially controversial issues. . . . The result is often the subjugation of the nation's common welfare.
—NANCY KASSEBAUM

• • •

Do not run a campaign that would embarrass your mother.
—ROBERT BYRD

• • •

The only thing we learn from new elections is we learned nothing from the old.
—AMERICAN PROVERB

• • •

There is nothing wrong with this country
that a good election can't fix.
—RICHARD NIXON

• • •

Our elections are free—it's the results where
we eventually pay.
—BILL STERN

• • •

Ninety-eight percent of the adults in this country are decent,
hard-working, honest Americans. It's the other lousy two
percent that get all the publicity. But then, we elected them.
—LILY TOMLIN

• • •

One of the nuisances of the ballot is that when the oracle has
spoken you never know what it means.
—LORD SALISBURY

• • •

An election is coming. Universal peace is declared, and the foxes have a sincere interest in prolonging the lives of the poultry.
—GEORGE ELIOT, pen name of MARY ANNE EVANS, *Felix Holt, the Radical* (1866)

• • •

I like the smell of a dunged field, and the tumult of a popular election.
—AUGUSTUS WILLIAM HARE and JULIUS CHARLES HARE, *Guesses at Truth, by Two Brothers* (1827)

• • •

The people have spoken—the bastards.
—DICK TUCK, after losing the 1966 California Senate election

• • •

There are two political truisms: Old people vote and Republicans eat their young.
—EDDIE WHITLOCK

• • •

Somebody asked me about the current choice we're being given in the presidential election. I said, well, it's like two of the scariest movies I can imagine.
—DEAN KOONTZ

• • •

The conduct of the Republican Party in his nomination is a remarkable indication of small intellect, growing smaller. They pass over . . . statesmen and able men, and they take up a fourth rate lecturer, who cannot speak good grammar.
—*NEW YORK HERALD*, on Abraham Lincoln's nomination for president

• • •

Every two years the American politics industry fills the airwaves with the most virulent, scurrilous, wall-to-wall character assassination of nearly every political practitioner in the country—and then declares itself puzzled that America has lost faith in its politicians.
—CHARLES KRAUTHAMMER, quoted in *Common Ground: How to Stop the Partisan War That Is Destroying America* by Cal Thomas and Bob Beckel (2007)

• • •

But I hope people understand this, your friends who like Obamacare, you remind them of this, if they want more stuff from government tell them to go vote for the other guy—more free stuff.
—MITT ROMNEY

• • •

I think it's been the worst campaign I've ever seen in my life. I hate that people think compromise is a dirty word. It's not a dirty word.
—BARBARA BUSH, in reference to the 2012 Republican presidential campaign

• • •

Liberals and Conservatives

A conservative is someone who stands athwart history, yelling, "Stop" at a time when no one is inclined to do so, or to have much patience with those who so urge it.
—WILLIAM F. BUCKLEY JR.

• • •

Should any political party attempt to abolish social security, unemployment insurance, and eliminate labor laws and farm programs, you would not hear of that party again in our political history. There is a tiny splinter group, of course, that believes you do these things. Among them are H. L. Hunt (you possibly know his background), a few other Texas oil millionaires, and an occasional politician or businessman from other areas. Their number is negligible and they are stupid.
—DWIGHT EISENHOWER

• • •

Though they were Liberals they were not
democrats; nor yet infidels.
—ANTHONY TROLLOPE, *Phineas Redux* (1874)

• • •

A liberal is a man too broadminded to take
his own side in a quarrel.
—ROBERT FROST

• • •

Politics, it seems to me, for years, or all too long, has been
concerned with right or left instead of right or wrong.
—RICHARD ARMOUR

• • •

If there is a demon-of-all-demons for liberals,
it is Newt Gingrich.
—GEORGE LAKOFF, *Moral Politics: How Liberals and
Conservatives Think* (2002)

• • •

Maybe just because I grew up in a different time, but though I
often disagree with Republicans, I never learned to hate them
the way the far right that now controls their party seems to
hate President Obama and the Democrats.
—BILL CLINTON

• • •

Primaries

Primaried: 1. To have a wealthy backer provide support to someone who will publicly oppose and trash you, usually in politics, and usually from your own party.
—URBANDICTIONARY.COM

• • •

Each of the past few election cycles has featured at least one instance of "primarying," a challenge to an incumbent on the grounds that he or she is not sufficiently partisan. For many observers, such races signify an increasingly polarized electorate and an increasing threat to moderates of both parties.
—ROBERT G. BOATRIGHT, *Getting Primaried* (2013)

• • •

Despite what the pundits want us to think, contested primaries aren't civil war, they are democracy at work, and that's beautiful.
—SARAH PALIN

• • •

During a campaign the air is full of speeches—and vice versa.
—ANONYMOUS

• • •

During a political campaign everyone is concerned with what a candidate will do on this or that question if he is elected— except the candidate; he's too busy wondering what he'll do if he isn't elected.
—EVERETT DIRKSEN

• • •

The biggest difference was the way the two candidates spoke to voters: Romney spoke to job creators, businesses, large and small. Obama spoke to people who worked for businesses. As [Romney spokesman] Kevin Madden said: "We were doing economics and he was doing love songs."
—DAN BALZ

• • •

General Motors, General Mills, General Foods, general ignorance, general apathy, and general cussedness elect presidents and Congressmen and maintain them in power.
—HERBERT M. SHELTON

• • •

The theory is that election to Congress is tantamount to be being dispatched to Washington on a looting raid for the enrichment of your state or district and no other ethic need inhibit the feeding frenzy.
—GEORGE F. WILL

• • •

Voter apathy was, and will remain, the greatest threat to democracy.
—HAZEN S. PINGREE

• • •

Elections belong to the people. It's their decision. If they decide to turn their back on the fire and burn their behinds, then they will just have to sit on their blisters.
—ABRAHAM LINCOLN

• • •

Voting

[T]he question is no longer the academic one: "Is it wise to give every man the ballot?" But rather the practical one: "Is it prudent to deprive whole classes of it any longer?"
—JAMES RUSSELL LOWELL

• • •

Individual rights are not subject to a public vote; a majority has no right to vote away the rights of a minority: the political function of rights is precisely to protect minorities from oppression by majorities (and the smallest minority on earth is the individual).
—AYN RAND

• • •

Sensible and responsible women do not want to vote. The relative positions to be assumed by man and woman in the working out of our civilization were assigned long ago by a higher intelligence than ours.
—GROVER CLEVELAND

• • •

It would be a much better country if women did not vote. That is simply a fact. In fact, in every presidential election since 1950—except Goldwater in '64—the Republican would have won, if only the men had voted.
—ANN COULTER

• • •

American youth attributes much more importance to arriving at driver's license age than voting age.
—MARSHALL McLUHAN, *Understanding Media: The Extensions of Man* (1964)

• • •

Gerrymandering, also known as Redistricting

Redistricting has made a tiny slice of ideological activists the power brokers in who gets sent to Congress.
—NORMAN J. ORNSTEIN

• • •

The Republicans are going to have their hand on the computer mouse, and when you have your hand on the computer mouse, you can change a district from a "D" [Democratic] to an "R" [Republican].
—KIMBALL W. BRACE

Voter Fraud

Last month, police in Pontiac, Michigan, found the mummified body of Pia Farrenkopf in the garage of her foreclosed home. She had apparently been dead since 2008, but was listed as having voted in the 2010 election for governor.
—JOHN FUND

• • •

Could it be voter fraud? Sure, it could be voter fraud. Could it be an error on the part of a precinct person choosing the wrong person's name in the first place? It could be. We're looking at each of these individual cases.
—KIM WESTBROOK STRACH

• • •

Campaign Spending

A restriction on the amount of money a person or group
can spend on political communication during a campaign
necessarily reduces the quantity of expression by restricting
the number of issues discussed, the depth of their exploration,
and the size of the audience reached. This is because virtually
every means of communicating ideas in today's mass society
requires the expenditure of money.
—*CATO HANDBOOK FOR CONGRESS*

• • •

[T]he Supreme Court issued a landmark decision supporting
free political speech by overturning some of Congress's more
intrusive limits on election spending.

Citizens United is in any event a bracing declaration that
Congress's long and misbegotten campaign-finance crusade
has reached a Constitutional dead end.
—*WALL STREET JOURNAL*

• • •

With its ruling today, the Supreme Court has given a green light to a new stampede of special interest money in our politics. It is a major victory for big oil, Wall Street banks, health insurance companies and the other powerful interests that marshal their power every day in Washington to drown out the voices of everyday Americans.

—BARACK OBAMA, response to US Supreme Court's *Citizens United* decision

• • •

CBS profit will climb by $180 million this year from political advertising, Chief Executive Officer Les Moonves said, exceeding the amount received by the company in the last presidential election year. "Super PACs may be bad for America," Moonves said, "but they're very good for CBS."

—ANDY FIXMER

• • •

It's a lot of money. Every presidential election is the most expensive ever. Elections don't get cheaper.

—ELLEN WEINTRAUB

• • •

Traditional liberals should be cheering the Supreme Court's decision last week in *McCutcheon v. Federal Election Commission*, which reaffirmed a value at the heart of the First Amendment: The best response to unwelcome or controversial political speech is more political speech.
—JEFF JACOBY

• • •

At the core of the disaster that is the Supreme Court's *McCutcheon v. FEC* decision lies a mistake. A strategic mistake, made by government. In this mistake, we can see all that's wrong with modern American constitutional law.
—LAWRENCE LESSIG

• • •

The idea that a congressman would be tainted by accepting money from private industry or private sources is essentially a socialist argument.
—NEWT GINGRICH

• • •

Do you ever get the feeling that only reason we have elections is to find out if the polls were right.
—ROBERT ORBEN

Chapter 3

The Legislative Branch

Whenever the legislators endeavor to take away the property of the people, or to reduce them to slavery under arbitrary power, they put themselves into a state of war with the people, who are thereupon absolved from any farther obedience, and are left to the common refuge which God hath provided for all men against force and violence.

—JOHN LOCKE

• • •

The rich, the well born, and the able, acquire an influence among the people that will soon be too much for simple honesty and plain sense, in a house of representatives. The most illustrious of them must, therefore, be separated from the mass, and placed by themselves in a senate; this is, to all honest and useful intents, an ostracism.
—JOHN ADAMS, *The Works of John Adams*,
vol. 4 (1851)

• • •

They [two fellow Congressmen] never open their mouths without subtracting from the sum of human knowledge.
—THOMAS BRACKETT REED, *The Life of*
Thomas Reed (1914)

• • •

Do you pray for the Senators, Dr. Hale? someone asked, No, I look at the Senators and I pray for our country.
—REVEREND EDWARD E. HALE

• • •

The Senate is an unknowing world.
—ROBERT CARO

• • •

Chris Christie also lashed out at Congress for doing nothing for the victims of Hurricane Sandy. But in their defense Congress says, "Hey, we don't do anything for anybody."
—JAY LENO

• • •

I have wondered at times what the Ten Commandments would have looked like if Moses had run them through the US Congress.
—RONALD REAGAN

• • •

People said the old deal was that all these people from agricultural districts are just going to vote for a farm bill. Well, no, I'm not going to go for 80 percent for food stamps to get the 20 percent for us.
—TIM HUELSKAMP, voting against a proposed 2013 farm bill

• • •

There's a whole herd of sacred cows grazing in the lush green pastures of the federal government. Even though many of them quit giving milk long ago, we still fund them. I say take 'em out and shoot 'em.
—ZELL MILLER

• • •

We don't want to turn the safety net into a hammock that lulls able-bodied people into complacency and dependence.
—PAUL RYAN

• • •

Looking at Capitol Hill is like looking at that Escher picture of the wild geese flying together: makes no fucking sense and occasionally shits on your head.
—DENNIS MILLER

• • •

Madam Speaker, this is a huge cow patty with a piece of marshmallow stuck in the middle of it, and I'm not going to eat that cow patty.
—PAUL BROUN, on the Dodd–Frank Wall Street Reform and Consumer Protection Act

• • •

Never to the knowledge of the undersigned [Republican Senators] has such vile, contemptible, inflammatory, and dangerous language been uttered in a campaign for the purpose of procuring nomination and election by an incumbent and member of the United States Senate, sworn to uphold the Constitution.

—REPUBLICAN MINORITY COMMITTEE
REPORT, urging exclusion of Mississippi Senator
Theodore Bilbo, a Democrat, for racist remarks in his
1946 re-election

• • •

I was ecstatic when they re-named "French fries" as "freedom fries." Grown men and women in positions of power in the US government showing themselves as idiots.

—JOHNNY DEPP (attributed), on Congress's reaction
to the French opposition to the US invasion of Iraq

• • •

Representative democracy requires electoral competition and the dependence of legislators on the people. But electoral competition is no longer possible in a system where the benefits and power of incumbency virtually guarantee a lifelong career as a legislator. The problem is not individual incumbents, but rather, chronic incumbency.
—MARK P. PETRACCA

• • •

I am persuaded that in the case of Congress, the overwhelming temptation is to conclude that it is more important for your constituents that you be reelected than to deal honestly with them.
—JAMES L. BUCKLEY

• • •

Asking an incumbent member of Congress to vote for (congressional) term limits is a bit like asking a chicken to vote for Colonel Sanders.
—BOB INGLIS

• • •

I have never seen more senators express discontent with their jobs. I think the major cause is that, deep down in our hearts, we have been accomplices to doing something terrible and unforgivable to this wonderful country. Deep down in our hearts, we know that we have bankrupted America and that we have given our children a legacy of bankruptcy. . . . We have defrauded our country to get ourselves elected.
—JOHN DANFORTH

• • •

Of all the reforms the freshmen [congressmen] wanted to bring to Washington, I believed setting term limits was by far the most important. Nothing would change the culture, the policies, more than replacing career politicians with citizen legislators. Political careerism, more than anything else, has separated Washington from the people. Careerism perpetuates big government and is a constant corrupting force in the system.
—TOM COBURN

• • •

Nothing is more important today than reversing the pernicious rise of a professional political class.
—DOUG BANDOW

• • •

Americans know real change in Washington will never happen until we end the era of permanent politicians. As long as members of Congress have the chance to spend their lives in Washington, their interests will always skew toward spending taxpayer dollars to pay off special interest supporters, covering over corruption in the bureaucracy, fund-raising, relationship-building with lobbyists, and trading favors for pork; in short, amassing their own power.
—JIM DEMINT

• • •

Yes, we need to raise the debt limit at some point, but we have to do it in the context of getting the spending under control. The president says we need to pay our bills. He [President Obama] misses the whole point. The point is we need to adjust what bills we're paying and how we're paying them.
—ROB PORTMAN

• • •

Allow a government to decline paying its debts and you overthrow all public morality—you unhinge all the principles that preserve the limits of free constitutions. Nothing can more affect national prosperity than a constant and systematic attention to extinguish the present debt and to avoid as much as possibly the incurring of any new debt.
—ALEXANDER HAMILTON

• • •

I don't mind what Congress does, as long as they don't do it in the streets and frighten the horses.
—VICTOR HUGO (attributed)

• • •

Some of them are valedictorians—and their parents brought them in. It wasn't their fault. It's true in some cases, but they aren't all valedictorians. They weren't all brought in by their parents. . . . For everyone who's a valedictorian, there's another 100 out there who weigh 130 pounds—and they've got calves the size of cantaloupes because they're hauling 75 pounds of marijuana across the desert. Those people would be legalized with the same act.
—STEVE KING, on his opposition to proposed immigration reform

• • •

In July 2012, GOP Iowa Congressman Steve King opposed a farm bill provision against animal fighting. He received a score of zero on the 2012 Humane Society Legislative Fund's Humane Scorecard. Afterwards, he put out a video clarifying his position where he defended his position by stating that it "would be putting animals above humans if it was legal to watch humans fight, but not animals."
—WIKIPEDIA.ORG, "Steve King"

• • •

The 112th [Congress], which ended January 3, [2013,] passed 220 laws, the fewest of any Congress since they started keeping statistics [in 1948], and more than 100 fewer than the previous record low. Yet, six months into its term the 113th Congress is actually on pace to pass even fewer laws than that.
—DASHIELL BENNETT

• • •

People say if the Congress were more representative of the people it would be better. I say the Congress is too damn representative. It's just as stupid as the people are; just as uneducated, just as dumb, just as selfish. You know the Congress is a perfect example, and created to be a perfect example.
—DEAN ACHESON

• • •

In January 2013, [n]inety-four newly elected members joined the 113th Congress. [Their] estimated median net worth is almost exactly $1 million more than that of the typical American household.
—OPENSECRETS.ORG, Congressional net worth data

• • •

I'm no lady; I'm a member of Congress, and I'll proceed on that basis.
—MARY TERESA NORTON

• • •

Senate Appropriations Committee Chairwoman [Barbara] Mikulski, a Maryland Democrat, intimidates people in a way that the two most recent committee chairmen, the late Senators Robert C. Byrd of West Virginia and Daniel K. Inouye of Hawaii, did not. During a March floor debate, Ms. Mikulski ordered Senator John McCain of Arizona to go back to his office and read a bill so he could properly vote on it—and Mr. McCain, chastened but cheerful, agreed. "I will now try to carry out my mission as assigned by the distinguished chairwoman," he said.

—JENNIFER STEINHAUER

• • •

Partisans

[M]any do not dare argue against them; on the contrary, they flatter them in order not to seem "conservative."
—ALEKSANDR SOLZHENITSYN

• • •

The modern conservative is engaged in one of man's oldest exercises in moral philosophy; that is, the search for a superior moral justification for selfishness.
—JOHN KENNETH GALBRAITH

• • •

The whole modern world has divided itself into Conservatives and Progressives. The business of Progressives is to go on making mistakes. The business of the Conservatives is to prevent the mistakes from being corrected.
—G. K. CHESTERTON

• • •

It is a fact that reality has a liberal bias.
—STEPHEN COLBERT

• • •

The radical of one country is the conservative of the next. The radical invents the views. When he has worn them out, the conservative adopts them.
—MARK TWAIN, *Notebook* (1935)

• • •

Extremes to the right and to the left of any political dispute are always wrong.
—DWIGHT EISENHOWER

• • •

Liberalism should surely be a passionate conviction. Liberals are not necessarily lukewarm. Only the more macho leftist suspects that they have no balls. You can be ardently neutral, and fiercely indifferent.
—TERENCE EAGLETON

• • •

The principal feature of American liberalism is sanctimoniousness. By loudly denouncing all bad things—war and hunger and date rape—liberals testify to their own terrific goodness. More important, they promote themselves to membership in a self-selecting elite of those who care deeply about such things.
—P. J. O'ROURKE, *Give War a Chance* (1992)

• • •

I believe in a relatively equal society, supported by institutions that limit extremes of wealth and poverty. I believe in democracy, civil liberties, and the rule of law. That makes me a liberal, and I'm proud of it.
—PAUL KRUGMAN, *The Conscience of a Liberal* (2007)

• • •

What the liberal really wants is to bring about change that will not in any way endanger his position.
—STOKELY CARMICHAEL

• • •

House Republicans passed a budget resolution Thursday with an added amendment that defunds ObamaCare. To avoid a shutdown they'll fund the government for two weeks at a time. The US Congress that was designed by James Madison and descended from the House of Commons and Lords now has the financial planning skills of a college sophomore.
—ARGUS HAMILTON

• • •

When fascism comes to America, it will be wrapped in the flag, carrying a cross.
—SINCLAIR LEWIS

• • •

To their cost, American conservatives have forgotten Winston Churchill's famous distinction between left and right—that the left favors the line, the right the ladder. Democrats do indeed support policies that encourage voters to line up for entitlements—policies that often have the unintended consequence of trapping recipients in dependency on the state. Republicans need to start reminding people that conservatism is about more than just cutting benefits. It's supposed to be about getting people to climb the ladder of opportunity.

—DAVID FRUM

• • •

A conservative is one who admires radicals centuries after they're dead.

—LEO ROSTEN

• • •

Conservatives must take note of those Republicans who betrayed our movement today.

—DAVID BOSSIE, responding to US Senate passing immigration reform legislation, with support of Republican Senators

• • •

The only difference between the Democrats and the
Republicans is that the Democrats allow
the poor to be corrupt too.
—OSCAR LEVANT

• • •

Republicans believe every day is the Fourth of July, but the
democrats believe every day is April 15.
—RONALD REAGAN

• • •

The Democrats seem to be basically nicer people, but
they have demonstrated time and again that they have the
management skills of celery.
—DAVE BARRY

• • •

We now see all too clearly that the hope and change the Democrats had in mind was nothing more than a retread of the failed and discredited socialist policies that have been the enemy of freedom for centuries all over the world. . . . The federal government is assaulting almost every sector of our free market economy. . . . I fear America is teetering towards tyranny.
—JIM DEMINT

• • •

History tells us that American liberals have long underestimated the reach and resilience of the right, repeatedly dismissing it as a lunatic fringe and pronouncing it dead only to watch it bounce back stronger after each setback.
—FRANK RICH

• • •

Filibusters and Other Legislative Tactics

Filibuster, *noun*: the use of extreme dilatory tactics in an attempt to delay or prevent action especially in a legislative assembly; an instance of such action.
—MERRIAM-WEBSTER'S COLLEGIATE DICTIONARY

• • •

The whole idea . . . is that you could have a minority . . . willing to debate around the clock, to sleep on mattresses outside the chamber, to take the issue to the country.

What's happened since the rule's change, and especially in the last few years, is you don't have to do any of that. You lift your little finger and say, "I intend to filibuster," . . . to stop that process, the majority needs to produce 60 votes.
—NORMAN J. ORNSTEIN and THOMAS E. MANN, *It's Even Worse Than It Looks* (2012)

• • •

The only thing more depressing than democracy at work is democracy not allowed to.
—P. J. O'ROURKE

• • •

Our representative democracy is not working, because the Congress that is supposed to represent the voters does not respond to their needs. I believe the chief reason for this is that it is ruled by a small group of old men.
—SHIRLEY CHISHOLM, *Chisholm '72: Unbought and Unbossed* (1970)

• • •

I yield to no man in my belief in the principle of free debate, inside or outside the halls of Congress. The sound of tireless voices is the price we pay for the right to hear the music of our own opinions. But there is also, it seems to me, a moment at which democracy must prove its capacity to act. Every man has a right to be heard; but no man has the right to strangle democracy with a single set of vocal cords.
—ADLAI E. STEVENSON II

• • •

Money, Money, Money

In the 2012 election 1,711 candidates were vying for 468 congressional seats—435 seats in the House, 33 in the Senate, and a record $3.67 billion was spent on congressional campaigns. That was $1 billion more than the total spent on the 2012 presidential races.
—CENTER FOR RESPONSIVE POLITICS

• • •

This is not one person doing one bad thing. You can't have a corrupt lobbyist unless you have a corrupt member [of Congress] or a corrupt staff. . . . This was a team effort.
—NEWT GINGRICH, on super-lobbyist Jack Abramoff's conviction on corruption, tax evasion, and fraud

• • •

Men who look upon themselves born to reign, and others to obey, soon grow insolent; selected from the rest of mankind their minds are early poisoned by importance; and the world they act in differs so materially from the world at large, that they have but little opportunity of knowing its true interests, and when they succeed to the government are frequently the most ignorant and unfit of any throughout the dominions.

—THOMAS PAINE, *Common Sense* (1776)

• • •

Congressional Scandals

It could probably be shown by facts and figures that there is no distinctly Native American criminal class except Congress.
—MARK TWAIN

• • •

On May 22, 1856, Representative Andrew Butler, of South Carolina, entered the Senate chamber and savagely beat Senator Charles Sumner, an avid antislavery Republican from Massachusetts, with a cane. Three days earlier, Sumner, in his "Crime Against Kansas" speech in opposition to admission of Kansas to the Union as a slave state, proclaimed that Butler had taken "the harlot, Slavery" as his mistress.

After the attack, both men became heroes in their respective regions.
—SENATE.GOV, "The Caning of Charles Sumner"

• • •

A fondness for power is implanted, in most men, and it is
natural to abuse it, when acquired.
—ALEXANDER HAMILTON

• • •

A California congressman helped secure tax breaks for
racehorse owners—then purchased seven horses for himself
when the new rules kicked in. A Wyoming congresswoman
co-sponsored legislation to double the life span of federal
grazing permits that ranchers such as her
husband rely on to feed cattle.
The practice is both legal and permitted under the ethics rules
that Congress has written for itself, which allow lawmakers to
take actions that benefit themselves or their families except
when they are the lone beneficiaries. The financial disclosure
system Congress has implemented also does not require the
legislators to identify potential conflicts at the time that they
take official actions that intersect or overlap
with their investments.
—KIMBERLY KINDY, DAVID S. FALLIS,
and SCOTT HIGHAM

• • •

The inside operation of Congress—the deals, the compromises, the selling out, the co-opting, the unprincipled manipulating, the self-serving career-building—is a story of such monumental decadence, I believe that if people find out about it they will demand an end to it.
—BELLA ABZUG

• • •

If the representatives of the people betray their constituents, there is then no recourse left but in the exertion of that original right of self-defense.
—ALEXANDER HAMILTON

• • •

Chapter 4

Presidents

The preservation of the sacred fire of liberty, and the destiny of the republican model of government, are justly considered as deeply, perhaps as finally staked, on the experiment entrusted to the hands of the American people.
—GEORGE WASHINGTON

• • •

First in war, first in peace, and first in the hearts of his countrymen.
—HENRY LEE III, eulogy at George Washington's funeral

• • •

The consequences arising from the continual accumulation of public debts in other countries ought to admonish us to be careful to prevent their growth in our own.
—JOHN ADAMS

• • •

The tree of liberty must be refreshed from time to time with the blood of patriots and tyrants. It is its natural manure.
—THOMAS JEFFERSON

• • •

A little rebellion now and then is a good thing.
—THOMAS JEFFERSON

• • •

Religion and Government will both exist in greater purity, the less they are mixed together.
—JAMES MADISON

• • •

The conflict between the principle of liberty and the fact of slavery is coming gradually to an issue. Slavery has now the power, and falls into convulsions at the approach of freedom.
—JOHN QUINCY ADAMS

• • •

All the public business in Congress now connects itself with intrigues, and there is great danger that the whole government will degenerate into a struggle of cabals.
—JOHN QUINCY ADAMS

• • •

Do they think that I am such a damned fool as to think myself fit for President of the United States? No, sir; I know what I am fit for. I can command a body of men in a rough way, but I am not fit to be President.
—ANDREW JACKSON, quoted in *The Life of Andrew Jackson* by James Parton (1860)

• • •

There is more selfishness and less principle among members of Congress, as well as others, than I had any conception [of], before I became President of the US.
—JAMES K. POLK

• • •

With me it is emphatically true that the presidency is "no bed of roses."
—JAMES K. POLK

• • •

These capitalists generally act harmoniously and in concert to fleece the people, and now that they have got into a quarrel with themselves, we are called upon to appropriate the people's money to settle the quarrel.
—ABRAHAM LINCOLN

• • •

Where slavery is, there liberty cannot be; and where liberty is, there slavery cannot be.
—ABRAHAM LINCOLN

• • •

Plainly, the central idea of secession is the essence of anarchy.
—ABRAHAM LINCOLN

• • •

When [I] hear anyone arguing for slavery, I feel a strong impulse to see it tried on him personally.
—ABRAHAM LINCOLN

• • •

I feel incompetent to perform duties so important and responsible as those which have been so unexpectedly thrown upon me.
—ANDREW JOHNSON, first address to his cabinet after assuming office following President Lincoln's assassination

• • •

God gave us Lincoln and Liberty, let us fight for both.
—ULYSSES S. GRANT, toast prior to the Vicksburg Campaign

• • •

My policy is trust, peace, and to put aside the bayonet.
—RUTHERFORD B. HAYES

• • •

The President is the last person in the world to know what the people really want and think.
—JAMES A. GARFIELD, quoted in *Garfield of Ohio: The Available Man* by John M. Tyler (1970)

• • •

Ma, Ma, where's my Pa?
—1984 REPUBLICAN CAMPAIGN CHANT, after
Grover Cleveland acknowledged paying child support
to Maria Crofts Halpin, who claimed he fathered her
child Oscar Folsom Cleveland

• • •

Speak softly and carry a big stick; you will go far.
—THEODORE ROOSEVELT, phrase he used to
describe his own foreign policy, attributed to a West
African proverb

• • •

Our aim is not to do away with corporations. . . .We draw the
line against misconduct, not against wealth.
—THEODORE ROOSEVELT

• • •

Prosperity . . . is necessarily the first theme of
a political campaign.
—WOODROW WILSON

• • •

Once lead this people into war [World War II] and they will forget there ever was such a thing as tolerance.
—WOODROW WILSON

• • •

I am not fit for this office and should never have been here.
—WARREN G. HARDING, quoted in *Across the Busy Years* by Nicholas Murray Butler (1939)

• • •

The chief business of the American people is business.
—CALVIN COOLIDGE

• • •

The slog of progress is changing from the full dinner pail to the full garage.
—HERBERT HOOVER

• • •

Blessed are the young, for they shall inherit the national debt.
—HERBERT HOOVER

• • •

I pledge you, I pledge myself, to a new deal for the American people.
—FRANKLIN D. ROOSEVELT

• • •

On this 10th day of June, 1940, the hand that held the dagger has struck it into the back of its neighbor.
—FRANKLIN D. ROOSEVELT, on Italy's declaring war against France

• • •

Yesterday, December 7, 1941—a date which will live in infamy—the United States of America was suddenly and deliberately attacked by naval and air forces of the Empire of Japan.
—FRANKLIN D. ROOSEVELT

• • •

I must admit Roosevelt's leadership has been very effective
and has been responsible for the Americans' advantageous
position today.
—KANTARO SUZUKI

• • •

Boys, if you ever pray, pray for me now. I've got the most
terribly responsible job a man ever had.
—HARRY S. TRUMAN, comment to reporters on
becoming the 33rd US President upon Roosevelt's death

• • •

This is a solemn but a glorious hour. I only wish that
Franklin D. Roosevelt had lived to witness this day. General
Eisenhower informs me that the forces of Germany have
surrendered to the United Nations. The flags of freedom fly
over all Europe.
—HARRY S. TRUMAN

• • •

Sixteen hours ago an American airplane dropped one bomb on Hiroshima and destroyed its usefulness to the enemy.

We are now prepared to obliterate more rapidly and completely every productive enterprise the Japanese have above ground in any city.
—HARRY S. TRUMAN

• • •

The White House is the finest jail in the world.
—HARRY S. TRUMAN

• • •

Neither a wise man nor a brave man lies down on the tracks of history to wait for the train of the future to run over him.
—DWIGHT EISENHOWER

• • •

In the councils of government, we must guard against the acquisition of unwarranted influence, whether sought or unsought, by the military-industrial complex. The potential for the disastrous rise of misplaced power exists and will persist.
—DWIGHT EISENHOWER

• • •

If more politicians knew poetry, and more poets knew politics, I am convinced the world would be a little better place in which to live.
—JOHN F. KENNEDY

• • •

And so, my fellow Americans: ask not what your country can do for you—ask what you can do for your country.
—JOHN F. KENNEDY

• • •

Surely, in 1963, one hundred years after Emancipation, it should not be necessary for any American citizen to demonstrate in the streets for the opportunity to stop at a hotel, or to eat at a lunch counter in the very department store in which he is shopping, or to enter a motion picture house, on the same terms as any other customer.
— JOHN F. KENNEDY, special message to Congress on civil rights and job opportunities

• • •

You certainly can't say that the people of Dallas haven't given you a nice welcome, Mr. President.

—NELLIE CONNALLY, comment to President
Kennedy moments before he was assassinated

• • •

There's so much bitterness I thought they would get one of us, but Jack, after all he'd been through, never worried about it.

—ROBERT F. KENNEDY, hours after JFK's
assassination, quoted in *Brothers* by David Talbot (2007)

• • •

Let us close the springs of racial poison. Let us pray for wise and understanding hearts. Let us lay aside irrelevant differences and make our Nation whole.

—LYNDON B. JOHNSON, in an address to the nation
on signing the Civil Rights Bill

• • •

We are not about to send American boys nine or ten thousand miles away from home to do what Asian boys ought to be doing for themselves.

—LYNDON B. JOHNSON

• • •

I don't want loyalty. I want *loyalty*. I want him to kiss my ass in Macy's window at high noon and tell me it smells like roses. I want his pecker in my pocket.
—LYNDON B. JOHNSON, on a prospective assistant, quoted in *The Best and the Brightest* by David Halberstam (1972)

• • •

He's [Richard Nixon] like a Spanish horse, who runs faster than anyone for the first nine lengths and then turns around and runs backwards. You'll see; he'll do something wrong in the end. He always does.
—LYNDON B. JOHNSON

• • •

When the President does it, that means that it is not illegal.
—RICHARD NIXON

• • •

[J]ust think how much you're going to be missing. You don't have Nixon to kick around any more. Thank you, gentlemen, and good day.
—RICHARD NIXON

• • •

I don't give a shit what happens. I want you all to stonewall it, let them plead the Fifth Amendment, cover up or anything else, if it'll save it, save this plan. That's the whole point. We're going to protect our people if we can.
—RICHARD NIXON

• • •

We must maintain the integrity of the White House, and that integrity must be real, not transparent. There can be no whitewash at the White House.
—RICHARD NIXON

• • •

Well, I'm not a crook. I've earned everything I've got.
—RICHARD NIXON

• • •

And I want you to know that I have no intention whatever of ever walking away from the job that the people elected me to do for the people of the United States.
—RICHARD NIXON

• • •

To leave office before my term is completed is abhorrent to
every instinct in my body. But as President I must put the
interests of America first. America needs a full-time President
and a full-time Congress, particularly at this time with
problems we face at home and abroad. . . .
I have never been a quitter.
—RICHARD NIXON

• • •

My fellow Americans, our long national nightmare is over.
—GERALD R. FORD, in his address on assuming the
US presidency after Nixon's resignation

• • •

Any system of economics is bankrupt if it sees either value or
virtue in unemployment.
—JIMMY CARTER

• • •

For the first time in the history of our country the majority of
our people believe that the next five years will be
worse than the past five years.
—JIMMY CARTER

• • •

I can't deny I'm a better ex-president than I was a president.
—JIMMY CARTER

• • •

President Ronald Reagan won because he ran against Jimmy Carter. If he had run unopposed, he would have lost.
—MORT SAHL

• • •

The Battle for the mind of Ronald Reagan was like the trench warfare of World War I: never have so many fought so hard for such barren terrain.
—PEGGY NOONAN, *What I Saw at the Revolution* (1990)

• • •

The unpleasant sound [George H. W.] Bush is emitting as he traipses from one conservative gathering to another is a thin, tinny "arf"—the sound of a lapdog.
—GEORGE F. WILL

• • •

I want a kinder, gentler nation.
—GEORGE H. W. BUSH

• • •

I'm the one who will not raise taxes.... Read my lips: no new taxes.
—GEORGE H. W. BUSH

• • •

Today I am signing into law H.R. 2092, the "Torture Victim Protection Act of 1991." The United States must continue its vigorous efforts to bring the practice of torture and other gross abuses of human rights to an end wherever they occur.
—GEORGE H. W. BUSH

• • •

Hell, if you work for Bill Clinton, you go up down more times than a whore's nightgown.
—JAMES CARVILLE

• • •

Now, I don't have all the answers, but I do know the old ways don't work. Trickledown economics has sure failed. And big bureaucracies, both private and public, they've failed too.
—BILL CLINTON

• • •

Indeed, I did have a relationship with Miss Lewinsky that was not appropriate. In fact, it was wrong.
—BILL CLINTON

• • •

Rarely is the question asked: is our children learning?
—GEORGE W. BUSH

• • •

I will have a foreign-handed foreign policy.
—GEORGE W. BUSH

• • •

To those of you who received honors, awards, and distinctions, I say well done. And to the C students, I say you, too, can be president of the United States.
—GEORGE W. BUSH

• • •

Today we've had a national tragedy. Two airplanes have crashed into the World Trade Center in an apparent terrorist attack on our country.
—GEORGE W. BUSH

• • •

States like these, and their terrorist allies, constitute an "axis of evil" aiming to threaten the peace of the world.
—GEORGE W. BUSH

• • •

You may not agree with some tough decisions I have made. But I hope you can agree that I was willing to make the tough decisions.
—GEORGE W. BUSH

• • •

Washington is shifting the burden of bad choices today onto the backs of our children and grandchildren. America has a debt problem and a failure of leadership. Americans deserve better.
—BARACK OBAMA

• • •

So what they are going to try to do is make you scared of me. You know he—oh, he's not patriotic enough. He's got a funny name. You know, he doesn't look like all of those other presidents on those dollar bills.

—BARACK OBAMA

• • •

An absence of hope can rot a society from within.

—BARACK OBAMA

• • •

They call it Armageddon, the end of freedom as we know it. After I signed the bill, I looked around to see if there were any asteroids falling, some cracks opening up in the earth. Turned out it was a nice day.

—BARACK OBAMA, after signing the
Affordable Care Act

• • •

Tonight, I can report to the American people and to the world that the United States has conducted an operation that killed Osama bin Laden, the leader of al-Qaeda, and a terrorist who's responsible for the murder of thousands of innocent men, women, and children.

—BARACK OBAMA

• • •

What we're not for is negotiating with people with a bomb strapped to their chest. We're not going to do that.
—DAN PFEIFFER, before Congressional deadlock over raising national debt limit caused the shutdown of non-essential government services and the furlough of 8,000 government workers

• • •

[If] he [Barack Obama] is elected president, then the radical Islamists, the al-Qaida, the radical Islamists and their supporters, will be dancing in the streets in greater numbers than they did on September 11.
—STEVE KING

• • •

Vice Presidents

Once there were two brothers: one ran away to sea, the other was elected Vice President—and nothing was ever heard from either of them again.
—THOMAS RILEY MARSHALL

• • •

The second office of this government is honorable and easy, the first is but a splendid misery.
—THOMAS JEFFERSON

• • •

I do not propose to be buried until I am dead.
—DANIEL WEBSTER, on turning down the vice presidency (1839)

• • •

The vice presidency is not worth a bucket of warm piss and the worst damn fool mistake I ever made.
—JOHN NANCE GARNER IV

• • •

Look at all the vice presidents in history. Where are they?
They were about as useful as a cow's fifth teat.
—HARRY S. TRUMAN

• • •

The vice presidency is sort of like the last cookie on the plate.
Everybody insists he won't take it, but somebody always does.
—BILL VAUGHAN

• • •

Democracy means that anyone can grow up to be president,
and anyone who doesn't grow up can be vice president.
—JOHNNY CARSON

• • •

Vice President Cheney has been the most dangerous vice
president we've had probably in American history.
—JOE BIDEN

• • •

Chapter 5

Justice

Let justice be done, though the heavens may fall.
—LATIN PROVERB, popularized
by WILLIAM MURRAY

• • •

I have always found that mercy bears richer
fruits than strict justice.
—ABRAHAM LINCOLN

• • •

It is better that ten guilty persons escape, than that one
innocent suffer.
—SIR WILLIAM BLACKSTONE

• • •

Justice is not a prize tendered to the good-natured, nor is it to be withheld from the ill-bred.
—CHARLES L. AARONS

• • •

Justice renders to every one his due. . . . Justice extorts no reward, no kind of price: she is sought, therefore, for her own sake.
—CICERO, *De Legibus* (*On the Laws*) (c. 43 BC)

• • •

You condemn on hearsay evidence alone, your sins increase.
—ANONYMOUS AFRICAN PROVERB

• • •

Every individual of the community at large has an equal right to the protection of government.
—ALEXANDER HAMILTON

• • •

The judicial power ought to be distinct from both the
legislative and executive, and independent upon both, that so
it may be a check upon both, as both should
be checks upon that.
—JOHN ADAMS

• • •

The Law

The law is reason free from passion.
—ARISTOTLE

• • •

The more corrupt the state, the more numerous the laws.
—TACITUS, *Annals* (117)

• • •

Nobody has a more sacred obligation to obey the law than
those who make the law.
—SOPHOCLES

• • •

Laws grind the poor, and rich men rule the law.
—OLIVER GOLDSMITH, *The Traveller* (1764)

• • •

Laws are the spider webs through which the big flies pass and the little ones get caught.
—HONORÉ DE BALZAC

• • •

What do I care about the law? Hain't I got the power?
—CORNELIUS "COMMODORE" VANDERBILT

• • •

Equal laws protecting equal rights . . . the best guarantee of loyalty and love of country.
—JAMES MADISON

• • •

I would be the first to advocate obeying just laws. One has not only a legal but a moral responsibility to obey just laws. Conversely, one has a moral responsibility to disobey unjust laws. I would agree with St. Augustine that "an unjust law is no law at all."
—DR. MARTIN LUTHER KING JR.

• • •

The law cannot save those who deny it, but neither can the law serve any who do not use it. The history of injustice and inequality is a history of disuse of the law. Law has not failed—and is not failing. We as a nation have failed ourselves by not trusting the law and by not using the law to gain sooner the ends of justice which law alone serves.
—LYNDON B. JOHNSON

• • •

The rule of law can be wiped out in one misguided, however well intentioned, generation. And if that should happen, it could take a century of striving and ordeal to restore it, and then only at the cost of the lives of many good men and women.
—WILLIAM T. GOSSETT

• • •

An unconstitutional act is not law; it confers no rights; it imposes no duties; affords no protection; it creates no office; it is in legal contemplation, as inoperative as though it had never been passed.
—STEPHEN J. FIELD

• • •

I think it can be shown that the law makes ten criminals
where it restrains one.
—VOLTAIRINE DE CLEYRE

● ● ●

[N]o law, written or unwritten, can be understood without a
full knowledge of the facts out of which it arises, and to which
it is to be applied.
—LOUIS BRANDEIS

● ● ●

Lawyers

A countryman between two lawyers is
like a fish between two cats.
—BENJAMIN FRANKLIN

• • •

I don't want a lawyer to tell me what I cannot do; I hire him to
tell me how to do what I want to do.
—JOHN PIERPONT "J. P." MORGAN

• • •

The worse the society, the more law there will be. In Hell,
there will be nothing but law and due process will be
meticulously observed.
—GRANT GILMORE, *The Ages of
American Law* (1977)

• • •

We have the heaviest concentration of lawyers on Earth—one for every five hundred Americans.... Ninety percent of our lawyers serve 10 percent of our people. We are over-lawyered and under-represented.

—JIMMY CARTER

• • •

[T]here is one human institution that makes a pauper the equal of a Rockefeller, the stupid man the equal of an Einstein, and the ignorant man the equal of any college president. That institution, gentlemen, is a court.

—HARPER LEE, *To Kill a Mockingbird* (1960)

• • •

The Supreme Court

Congress cannot pass laws that are contrary to the
Constitution, and it is the role of the Judicial system to
interpret what the Constitution permits.
—JOHN MARSHALL

• • •

We are under a great Constitution, but the Constitution is
what the judges say it is.
—CHARLES EVAN HUGHES

• • •

The most stringent protection of free speech would not protect
a man in falsely shouting fire in a theatre and causing a panic.
—OLIVER WENDELL HOLMES

• • •

We conclude that in the field of public education the doctrine of "separate but equal" has no place. Separate educational facilities are inherently unequal.
—EARL WARREN, court decision declaring segregated public schools unconstitutional, *Brown v. Board of Education*

• • •

The right of one charged with crime to counsel may not be deemed fundamental and essential to fair trials in some countries, but it is in ours. This noble ideal cannot be realized if the poor man charged with crime has to face his accusers without a lawyer to assist him.
—HUGO BLACK

• • •

An unconditional right to say what one pleases about public affairs is what I consider to be the minimum guarantee of the First Amendment.
—HUGO BLACK

• • •

The right of privacy…is broad enough to encompass a woman's decision whether or not to terminate her pregnancy.
—HARRY BLACKMUN

• • •

The Court must be living in another world. Day by day, case by case, it is busy designing a Constitution for a country I do not recognize
—ANTONIN SCALIA

• • •

The Affordable Care Act's requirement that certain individuals pay a financial penalty for not obtaining health insurance may reasonably be characterized as a tax. Because the Constitution permits such a tax, it is not our role to forbid it, or to pass upon its wisdom or fairness.
—JOHN G. ROBERTS

Chapter 6

The Press and Other
News Media

Congress shall make no law prohibiting... or abridging the
freedom of speech, or of the press.
—THE FIRST AMENDMENT TO THE *UNITED
STATES CONSTITUTION*

• • •

A newspaper is the lowest thing there is!
—RICHARD J. DALEY

• • •

Some degree of abuse is inseparable from the proper use of everything; and in no instance is this more true, than in that of the press.

—JAMES MADISON, *Report on the Virginia Resolutions* (1799)

• • •

[A]nd were it left to me to decide whether we should have a government without newspapers, or newspapers without a government, I should not hesitate a moment to prefer the latter. But I should mean that every man should receive those papers and be capable of reading them.

—THOMAS JEFFERSON

• • •

A good newspaper, I suppose, is a nation talking to itself.

—ARTHUR MILLER

• • •

The newspaper is in all literalness the bible of democracy, the book out of which a people determines its conduct. It is the only serious book most people read. It is the only book they read every day.
—WALTER LIPPMANN

• • •

Freedom of the press is guaranteed only to those who own one.
—A. J. LIEBLING

• • •

Journalism largely consists of saying "Lord Jones Dead" to people who never knew Lord Jones was alive.
—G. K. CHESTERTON, *The Wisdom of Father Brown* (1914)

• • •

Every President should have the right to shoot two reporters a year—without explanation.
—HERBERT HOOVER

• • •

The man who reads nothing at all is better educated than the man who reads nothing but newspapers.
—THOMAS JEFFERSON

• • •

No self-respecting fish would be wrapped in a Murdoch newspaper.
—MIKE ROYKO, before resigning from the *Chicago Sun-Times* after Rupert Murdoch bought the paper in 1984

• • •

News is the first rough draft of history.
—BEN BRADLEE

• • •

The things that bother the press about a president will ultimately bother the country.
—DAVID HALBERSTAM

• • •

Our media and political system has turned into a mutual protection racket.
—BILL MOYERS

• • •

In the First Amendment, the Founding Fathers gave the free press the protection it must have to fulfill its essential role in our democracy. . . . The press was protected so that it could bare the secrets of government and inform the people.
—HUGO BLACK

• • •

Television and the New Media

Today's political campaigns function as collection agencies for broadcasters. You simply transfer money from contributors to television stations.
—BILL BRADLEY

• • •

We've got a real irony here. We have politicians selling access to something we all own—our government. And then we have broadcasters selling access to something we all own—our airwaves. It's a terrible system.
—NEWTON MINOW

• • •

Children can't achieve unless we raise their expectations and turn off the television sets.
—BARACK OBAMA

• • •

The new media environment created by the demise of traditional business models and the proliferation of journalistic outlets with strategies designed to attract niche audiences has intensified a focus on sensationalism and extremism and reinforced the tribal divisions between the [political] parties.
—NORMAN J. ORNSTEIN and THOMAS E. MANN

• • •

[T]he disruptive power of the Internet raises other profound questions about what journalism is becoming, about its essential character and values.
—BILL KELLER

• • •

The tea party movement would have been impossible to organize and coordinate without email and the Web.
—KARL ROVE

• • •

Four years ago, Barack Obama kicked off his presidential campaign on the steps of Illinois' Old State Capitol, speaking in front of thousands of supporters and a throng of media. Earlier this month [April 4, 2011], when he formally announced his reelection campaign, he did so without [a] public appearance, in an online video.

—SEEMA MEHTA

• • •

Overall, 39 percent of all American adults took part in some sort of political activity on a social networking site during the 2012 campaign.

—PEW RESEARCH CENTER

• • •

On the whole, the Internet is bad news for the old forms of politics and statecraft. Those of us who are puzzled by Nicolas Sarkozy's attitude to the Internet when he called it a new frontier, or Angela Merkel when she called it "neuland," should consider the seriousness of the Internet's dire challenges to old-fashioned statecraft.

—HARRY J. BENTHAM

• • •

But it should be said up front that the arrival of Twitter, along with the proliferation of media platforms that now deliver content to hungry, informed consumers, marks a vast improvement over an era when a small handful of sainted journalists interpreted political news for the masses.
—PETER HAMBY

• • •

Twitter is a mess for campaign coverage. It makes us small and it makes us pissed off and mean, because Twitter as a conversation is incredibly acerbic and cynical and we don't need more of that in coverage of politics, we need less.
—JOHN DICKERSON

• • •

This mad plunge into social media-driven journalism would be mildly diverting if it wasn't so dangerous to the future of news reporting. Hard-core media values—truth, accuracy, fairness, balance, perspective, objectivity—are being lost at precisely the wrong time.
—*THE AUSTRALIAN*, "Lost in the Twitterverse"

Chapter 7

War

Laws are silent in time of war.
—CICERO

• • •

They shall beat their swords into plowshares, and their spears
into pruning hooks: nation shall not lift up sword against
nation, neither shall they learn war anymore.
—ISAIAH 2:4

• • •

Wars begin when you will, but they do not
end when you please.
—NICCOLO MACHIAVELLI, *History of Florence*
(1521–1524)

• • •

Let him who desires peace, prepare for war.
—PUBLIUS FLAVIUS VEGETIUS RENATUS

• • •

Anyone who has ever looked into the glazed eyes of a soldier
dying on the battlefield will think hard before starting a war.
—OTTO VON BISMARCK

• • •

Too many Americans think wrestling is real and war is fake.
—BARRY CRIMMINS, *Never Shake Hands with
a War Criminal* (2004)

• • •

Never think that war, no matter how necessary, no matter how justified, is not a crime.

—ERNEST HEMINGWAY, quoted in *Treasury for the Free World* by Ben Raeburn (1946)

• • •

War will exist until that distant day when the conscientious objector enjoys the same reputation and prestige that the warrior does today.

—JOHN F. KENNEDY

• • •

The revolutionary war is a war of the masses; it can be waged only by mobilizing the masses and relying on them.

—MAO ZEDONG, *The Little Red Book* (1964)

• • •

American War of Independence

Vigorous measures at present would soon put an end to this rebellion. . . . When this army is ordered to act against them, they will soon be convinced that they are very insignificant when opposed to regular troops.
—THOMAS PITCAIRN

• • •

Thus, was the civil war begun and a victory, the fruits of it on the side of the Americans, whom Lord Sandwich had the folly and rashness to proclaim coward.
—HORACE WALPOLE, commenting after the British loss at the Battles of Lexington and Concord

• • •

Everything that is right or natural pleads for separation. The blood of the slain, the weeping voice of nature cries, 'Tis time to part.
—THOMAS PAINE, *Common Sense* (1776)

• • •

The hour is fast approaching, on which the honor and success of this army, and the safety of our bleeding country depend. Remember officers and soldiers that you are free men, fighting for the blessings of liberty—that slavery will be your portion, and that of your posterity, if you do not acquit yourselves like men.
—GEORGE WASHINGTON

• • •

I must study politics and war that my sons may have liberty to study mathematics and philosophy.
—JOHN ADAMS

American Civil War

Plainly, the central idea of secession is the essence of anarchy.
—ABRAHAM LINCOLN

• • •

If John Brown did not end the war that ended slavery, he did at least begin the war that ended slavery.
—FREDERICK DOUGLASS

• • •

It is rather for us to be here dedicated to the great task remaining before us—that from these honored dead we take increased devotion to that cause for which they here gave the last full measure of devotion—that we here highly resolve that these dead shall not have died in vain—that this nation, under God, shall have a new birth of freedom—and that government of the people, by the people, for the people, shall not perish from the earth.
—ABRAHAM LINCOLN

• • •

Civil wars leave nothing but tombs.
—ALPHONSE DE LAMARTINE

• • •

We have fought this fight as long as, and as well as, we know how. We have been defeated . . . we must accept the situation. These men must go home and plant a crop, and we must proceed to build up our country on a new basis.
—ROBERT E. LEE, on the morning he surrendered, quoted in *Lee at Appomattox* by Charles Francis Adams (1902)

• • •

Civil War: A conflict that cost more than ten billion dollars. For less than half, the freedom of all the four million slaves could have been purchased.
—CHARLES BEARD, *The Rise of American Civilization* (1927)

• • •

If war wrought vast ruins, it also produced the most
consummate and beneficent results for freedom and
humanity. The nationality of the country was permanently
settled; and National Union and National Liberty are facts that
will endure as long as republican institutions
flourish on the earth.
—GEORGE WASHINGTON WILLIAMS

• • •

World War I

My friend, you would not tell with such high zest
To children ardent for some desperate glory,
The old lie: Dulce et decorum est Pro patria mori.
[Translation: It is sweet and fitting to die for your country.]
—WILFRED OWEN, *Dulce et Decorum Est Pro
Patria Mori* (1918)

• • •

The United States must be neutral in fact as well as in
name... We must be impartial.
—WOODROW WILSON, message to the Senate at the
start of World War I

• • •

Our object now…is to vindicate the principles of peace and justice in the life of the world as against selfish and autocratic power and to set up amongst the really free and self-governed peoples of the world such a concert of purpose and of action as will henceforth insure the observance of those principles.

—WOODROW WILSON

• • •

The supreme test of the nation has come. We must all speak, act, and serve together!

—WOODROW WILSON

• • •

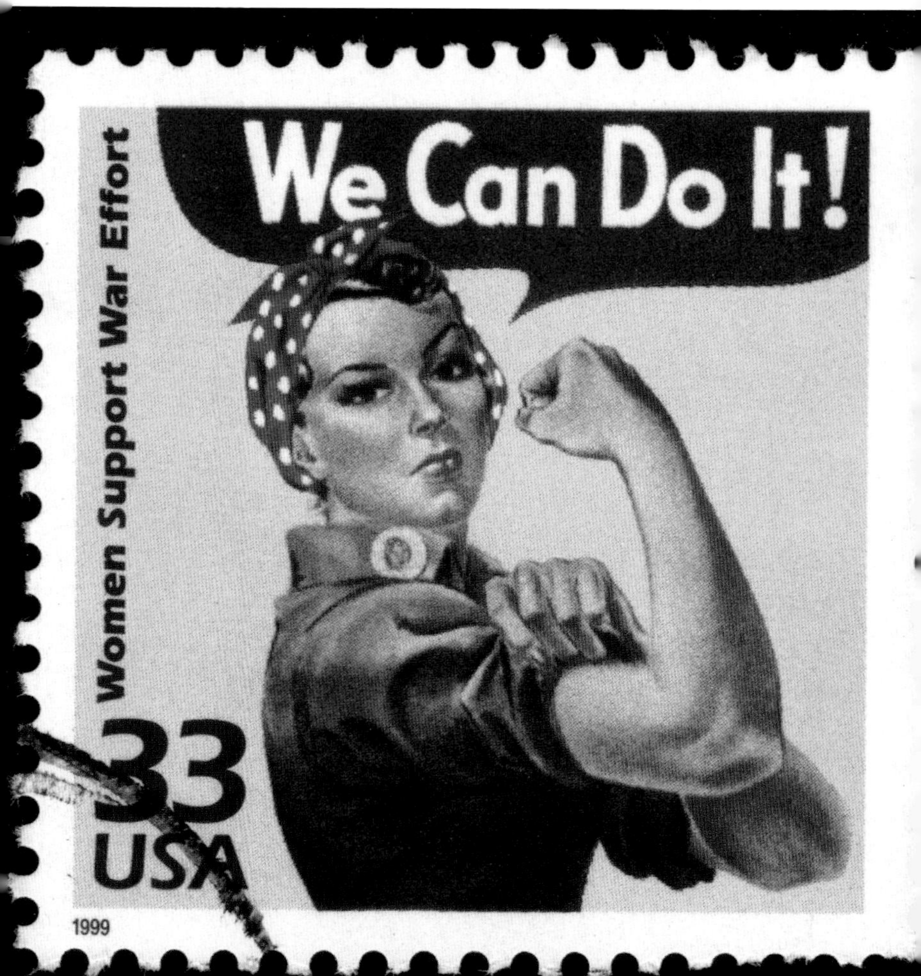

We Can Do It!
Women Support War Effort
33
USA
1999

World War II

Britain and France had to choose between war and dishonour.
They chose dishonour. They will have war.
—WINSTON CHURCHILL, criticizing Prime Minister
Neville Chamberlain in the House of Commons, after
the Munich accords

• • •

An appeaser is one who feeds a crocodile
hoping it will eat him last.
—WINSTON CHURCHILL

• • •

We have used it [the atomic bomb] against those who attacked
us without warning at Pearl Harbor, against those who
have starved and beaten and executed American prisoners
of war, against those who have abandoned all pretense of
obeying international laws of warfare. We have used it in
order to shorten the agony of war, in order to save the lives of
thousands and thousands of young Americans.
We shall continue to use it until we completely destroy Japan's
power to make war. Only a Japanese surrender will stop us.
—HARRY S. TRUMAN

• • •

I know not with what weapons World War III will be fought,
but World War IV will be fought with sticks and stones.
—ALBERT EINSTEIN

• • •

You can no more win a war than you can win an earthquake.
—JEANETTE RANKIN

• • •

The quickest way of ending a war is to lose it.
—GEORGE ORWELL, *Polemic* (1946)

• • •

We have grasped the mystery of the atom and rejected the Sermon on the Mount. . . . Ours is a world of nuclear giants and ethical infants. We know more about war than we know about peace, more about killing than we know about living.
—OMAR BRADLEY

• • •

Every gun that is made, every warship launched, every rocket fired signifies in the final sense, a theft from those who hunger and are not fed, those who are cold and are not clothed. This world in arms is not spending money alone. It is spending the sweat of its laborers, the genius of its scientists, the hopes of its children. This is not a way of life at all in any true sense. Under the clouds of war, it is humanity hanging on a cross of iron.
—DWIGHT EISENHOWER

• • •

The Korean War

Communism was acting in Korea, just as Hitler, Mussolini
and the Japanese had ten, fifteen, and twenty years earlier. . . .
If the Communists were permitted to force their way into the
Republic of Korea without opposition from the free world,
no small nation would have the courage to resist threat and
aggression by stronger Communist neighbors.
—HARRY S. TRUMAN, *The Autobiography of
Harry S. Truman* (1980)

• • •

Red China is not the powerful nation seeking to dominate
the world. Frankly, in the opinion of the Joint Chiefs of Staff,
this strategy would involve us in the wrong war, at the wrong
place, at the wrong time, and with the wrong enemy.
—OMAR BRADLEY, famous rebuke to General
MacArthur's proposal to extend Korean War into China

• • •

Retreat Hell! We're just attacking in another direction.
—OLIVER P. SMITH, remark during the Battle of
Chosin Reservoir

The Vietnam War

My solution to the problem [of North Vietnam] would be to tell them frankly that they've got to draw in their horns and stop their aggressiveness, or we're going to bomb them back into the Stone Age.

—CURTIS LEMAY, *Mission with LeMay: My Story* (1965)

• • •

We don't propose to sit here in our rocking chair with our hands folded and let the Communists set up any government in the Western Hemisphere.

—LYNDON B. JOHNSON

• • •

North Vietnam cannot defeat or humiliate the United States. Only Americans can do that.

—RICHARD NIXON

• • •

No event in American history is more misunderstood than the Vietnam War. It was misreported then, and it is misremembered now. Rarely have so many people been so wrong about so much. Never have the consequences of their misunderstanding been so tragic.

—RICHARD NIXON, *No More Vietnams* (1987)

• • •

I think Vietnam was what we had instead of happy childhoods.

—MICHAEL HERR, *Dispatches* (1977)

• • •

It does not take any courage at all for a congressman, or a senator, or a president to wrap himself in the flag and say we are staying in Vietnam, because it is not our blood that is being shed. But we are responsible for those young men and their lives and their hopes. And if we do not end this damnable war those young men will some day curse us for our pitiful willingness to let the Executive carry the burden that the Constitution places on us.

—GEORGE MCGOVERN

• • •

First Gulf War, Operation Desert Storm

Our strategy in going after this army is very simple. First we are going to cut it off, and then we are going to kill it.
—COLIN POWELL

• • •

The great duel, the mother of all battles has begun. . . . The dawn of victory nears as this great showdown begins!
—SADDAM HUSSEIN

• • •

As far as Saddam Hussein being a great military strategist: He is neither a strategist, nor is he schooled in the operational art, nor is he a tactician, nor is he a general, nor is he a soldier. Other than that, he's a great military man.
—H. NORMAN SCHWARZKOPF JR.

• • •

And it's my view that the President got it right both times, that it would have been a mistake for us to get bogged down in the quagmire inside Iraq.
—DICK CHENEY

• • •

Global War on Terror

Terrorism is the preferred weapon of weak and evil men.
—RONALD REAGAN

• • •

Terrorist attacks can shake the foundations of our biggest buildings, but they cannot touch the foundation of America. These acts shatter steel, but they cannot dent the steel of American resolve.
—GEORGE W. BUSH

• • •

I don't oppose all wars. What I am opposed to is a dumb war. What I am opposed to is a rash war. What I am opposed to is the cynical attempt by Richard Perle and Paul Wolfowitz and other armchair, weekend warriors in this administration to shove their own ideological agendas down our throats, irrespective of the costs in lives lost and in hardships borne. A dumb war. A rash war. A war based not on reason but on passion, not on principle but on politics.

—BARACK OBAMA

• • •

My fellow Americans: Major combat operations in Iraq have ended. In the battle of Iraq, the United States and our allies have prevailed.

—GEORGE W. BUSH

• • •

"Mission Accomplished."

—BANNER, backdrop for President George Bush's televised address from the USS *Abraham Lincoln*

• • •

The American people can take great pride in the way our military is treating these dangerous detainees. The [Geneva] Convention remains as important today as it was the day it was signed, and the United States is proud of its fifty-year history in compliance with the Convention.

—ARI FLEISCHER

• • •

There was no such thing as Al Qaeda in Iraq, until George Bush and John McCain decided to invade Iraq.

—BARACK OBAMA

• • •

For over the last decade, our nation has spent well over a trillion dollars on war, helping to explode our deficits and constraining our ability to nation-build here at home. Our service members and their families have sacrificed far more on our behalf. Nearly 7,000 Americans have made the ultimate sacrifice. Many more have left a part of themselves on the battlefield, or brought the shadows of battle back home. From our use of drones to the detention of terrorist suspects, the decisions that we are making now will define the type of nation—and world—that we leave to our children.

—BARACK OBAMA

Cyber Warfare

The NSA has built an infrastructure that allows it to intercept almost everything. With this capability, the vast majority of human communications are automatically ingested without targeting.

I don't want to live in a society that does these sort of things…I do not want to live in a world where everything I do and say is recorded. That is not something I am willing to support or live under.

—EDWARD SNOWDEN

• • •

He's [Snowden] obviously violated the laws of America…but I think the invasion of human rights and American privacy has gone too far. . . . I think that the secrecy that has been surrounding this invasion of privacy has been excessive, so I think that the bringing of it to the public notice has probably been, in the long term, beneficial.

—JIMMY CARTER

Chapter 8

Taxes, Taxation, Taxpayers

The people are hungry. It is because those in authority eat up
too much in taxes.
—LAO-TZU

• • •

Taxes grow without rain.
—JEWISH PROVERB

• • •

We have always considered taxes to be the sinews of the state.
—CICERO

• • •

Taxation and representation are inseparable.
—CHARLES PRATT

• • •

Taxation with representation ain't so hot either.
—GERALD BARZAN

• • •

There are no taxes on the wages of sin.
—MAE WEST

• • •

There is one passage in the Scriptures to which all the potentates of Europe seem to have given their unanimous assent and approbation, and to have studied so thoroughly as to have it quite at their fingers' ends [Luke 2:1]: "There went out a decree in the days of Claudius Caesar, that all the world should be taxed."
—CHARLES CALEB COLTON

• • •

The wisdom of man never yet contrived a system of taxation
that would operate with perfect equality.
—ANDREW JACKSON

• • •

People who complain about taxes can be divided into two
classes: men and women.
—ANONYMOUS

• • •

[A] heavy and heavily progressive inheritance tax on great
fortunes would be a far better thing.
—THEODORE ROOSEVELT

• • •

The only thing that hurts more than paying an income tax is
not having to pay an income tax.
—THOMAS ROBERT DEWAR

• • •

A government which robs Peter to pay Paul can always
depend on the support of Paul.
—GEORGE BERNARD SHAW, *Everybody's Political
What's What?* (1914)

• • •

I like to pay taxes. With them I buy civilization.
—OLIVER WENDELL HOLMES JR.

• • •

I'm proud to be paying taxes in the United States. The only thing is, I could be just as proud on half the money.
—ARTHUR GODFREY

• • •

Logic and taxation are not always the best of friends.
—JAMES C. McREYNOLDS

• • •

I don't know what to do, or where to turn in this taxation matter. Somewhere there must be a book that tells all about it, where I could go to straighten it out in my mind. But I don't know where the book is, and maybe I couldn't read it if I found it.
—WARREN G. HARDING, quoted in *The Shadow of Blooming Grove: Warren G. Harding in His Times* by Francis Russell (1968)

• • •

Thank goodness we don't get all of the government that we are made to pay for.
—MILTON FRIEDMAN

• • •

Intaxication: Euphoria at getting a refund from the IRS, which lasts until you realize it was your money to start with.
— *WASHINGTON POST* ANNUAL WORD CONTEST

• • •

Tax reform means: Don't tax you, don't tax me, tax that fellow behind the tree.
—RUSSELL B. LONG

• • •

The taxpayer—that's someone who works for the federal government but doesn't have to take a civil service examination.
—RONALD REAGAN

• • •

I was making a speech on the Senate floor and I said, "Now, gentlemen, let me tax your memories," and Kennedy jumped up and said, "Why haven't we thought of that before?"
—BOB DOLE

• • •

We contend that for a nation to try to tax itself into prosperity is like a man standing in a bucket and trying to lift himself up by the handle.
—WINSTON CHURCHILL

• • •

I don't want to abolish government. I simply want to reduce it to the size where I can drag it into the bathroom and drown it in the bathtub.
—GROVER NORQUIST

• • •

The rigidity of those pledges is something that I don't like. You know, the circumstances change and you can't be wedded to some formula by Grover Norquist. It's—who the hell is Grover Norquist, anyway?
—GEORGE H. W. BUSH

• • •

The Internal Revenue Service

For two years in a row, Congress has pared back the IRS
budget. . . . All told, IRS now has 5,000 fewer employees this
tax season than last . . . at the end of 2012, the IRS
workforce—97,717 employees—had dropped
9 percent from 2010 levels.
—JACK MOORE

• • •

[I]ndividuals and businesses spend about 6.1 billion hours a
year complying with tax-filing requirements. That adds up to
the equivalent of more than three million full-time workers,
or more than the number of jobs on the entire federal
government's payroll.
—CATHERINE RAMPELL

• • •

In 2012, the IRS answered just two-thirds of calls from taxpayers, and the average person who got through had to spend seventeen minutes on hold.

—IRS.GOV

• • •

Did you ever notice that when you put the words "The" and "IRS" together, it spells "THEIRS?"

—ANONYMOUS

• • •

April is the month when the green returns to the law, the trees, and the Internal Revenue Service.

—EVAN ESAR

• • •

Tax Deductions, Credits, Loopholes, and Cheats
An economy breathes through its tax loopholes.

—BARRY BRACEWELL-MILNES

• • •

Despite reporting net income of $30 billion over the four-year period 2009 to 2012, Apple Operations International paid no corporate income taxes to any national government during that period.
—US SENATE PERMANENT SUBCOMMITTEE ON INVESTIGATIONS, "Offshore Profit Shifting and the U.S. Tax Code-Part 2 (Apple Inc.)"

• • •

By shuffling his company stock in and out of more than thirty trusts, [Sheldon Adelson has] given at least $7.9 billion to his heirs while legally avoiding about $2.8 billion in US gift taxes since 2010.
—ZACHARY R. MIDER

• • •

[W]ealthy Americans who benefit hugely from a system rigged in their favor react with hysteria to anyone who points out just how rigged the system is. . . . [T]heir reaction to proposals to close a loophole that lets some of them pay remarkably low taxes—well, Stephen Schwarzman, chairman of the Blackstone Group, compared it to Hitler's invasion of Poland.
—PAUL KRUGMAN

If you don't drink, smoke, or drive a car, you're a tax evader.
—THOMAS S. FOLEY

• • •

We don't pay taxes. Only the little people pay taxes.
—LEONA HELMSLEY, real estate heiress convicted and
imprisoned for evading $1.7 million of taxes

• • •

H. Ty Warner . . . creator of Beanie Babies . . . was charged [in
September 2013] with hiding from his accountants and the
IRS over $3.1 million in foreign income generated
in a secret Swiss account.
—US ATTORNEY'S OFFICE, Northern
District of Illinois

• • •

If we don't do something to simplify the tax system, we're
going to end up with a national police force of internal
revenue agents.
—LEON PANETTA

• • •

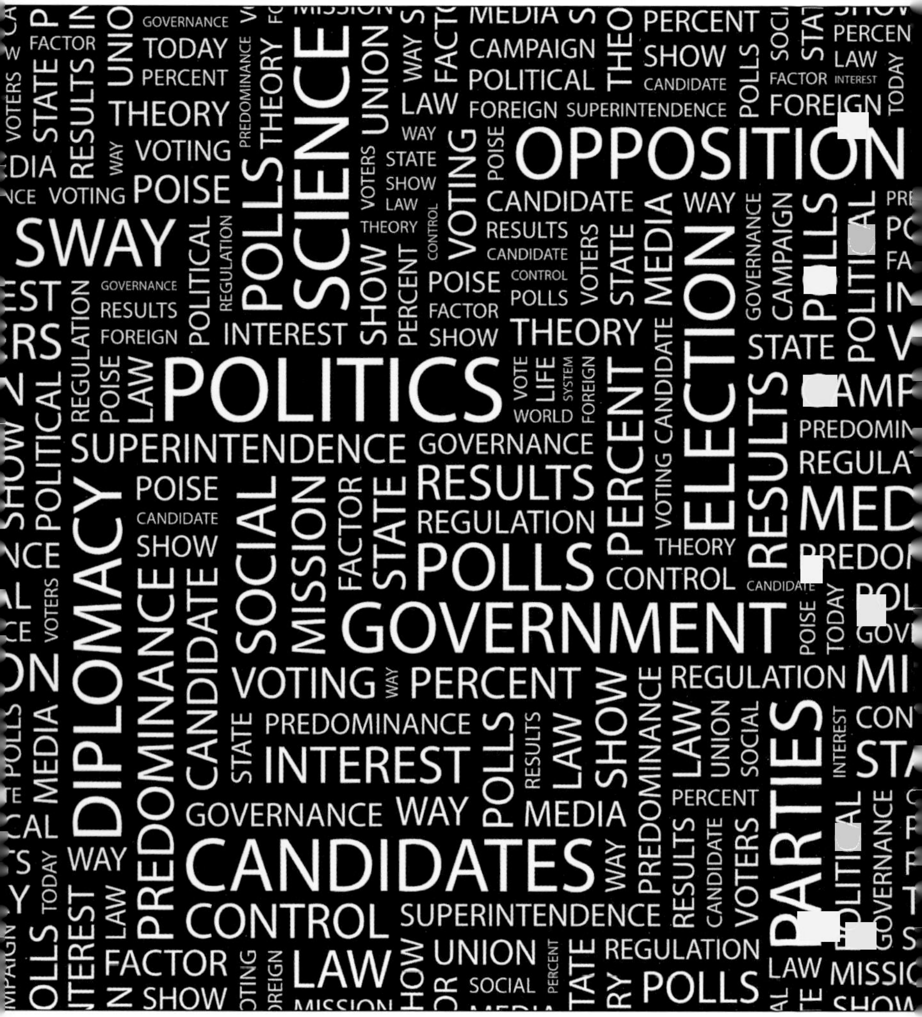
OPPOSITION
SCIENCE
SWAY
POLITICS
ELECTION
SUPERINTENDENCE
GOVERNANCE
RESULTS
REGULATION
POLLS
DIPLOMACY
SOCIAL
MISSION
GOVERNMENT
PARTIES
VOTING
PERCENT
PREDOMINANCE
INTEREST
CANDIDATES
CONTROL
LAW
THEORY
CAMPAIGN
POLITICAL
FOREIGN
MEDIA
CANDIDATE
POISE
FACTOR
SHOW
STATE
UNION
WAY
TODAY
VOTERS

Chapter 9

Economics and Economists

Economics is a study of mankind in the
ordinary business of life.
—ALFRED MARSHALL

• • •

If all the economists were laid end to end, they would not
reach a conclusion.
—GEORGE BERNARD SHAW

• • •

Most of economics, as taught, is a form of brain damage.
—ERNST F. SCHUMACHER, *Small Is Beautiful* (1973)

• • •

Economics is meant to be useful.
—RICHARD LAYARD and ALAN A. WALTERS

• • •

The economy depends about as much on economists as the weather does on weather forecasters.
—JEAN-PAUL KAUFFMANN

• • •

But while they prate of economic laws, men and women are starving. We must lay hold of the fact that economic laws are not made by nature. They are made by human beings.
—FRANKLIN ROOSEVELT

• • •

Economics is extremely useful as a form of employment for economists.
—JOHN KENNETH GALBRAITH

• • •

[S]ince consumption is merely a means to human well-being, the aim should be to obtain the maximum of well-being with the minimum of consumption.
—ERNST F. SCHUMACHER

• • •

Harry Truman once said he wanted a one-armed economist who didn't always say, "On the other hand."
—LAURENCE J. PETER

• • •

Ask five economists and you'll get five different answers—six if one went to Harvard.
—EDGAR RUSSELL FIEDLER

• • •

Ninety five per cent of economics is common sense deliberately made complicated.
—HA-JOON CHANG

• • •

Capitalism

Capitalism is the astounding belief that the most wicked of men will do the most wicked of things for the greatest good of everyone.
—JOHN MAYNARD KEYNES

• • •

I am now a Keynesian in economics.
—RICHARD NIXON, after taking the US off the gold standard

• • •

We have always known that heedless self-interest was bad morals; we know now that it is bad economics.
—FRANKLIN D. ROOSEVELT

• • •

The inherent vice of capitalism is the unequal sharing of blessings. The inherent virtue of socialism is the equal sharing of miseries.
—WINSTON CHURCHILL

• • •

The truth is we are all caught in a great economic system which is heartless.
—WOODROW WILSON

• • •

There is a serious tendency toward capitalism among the well-to-do peasants.
—MAO ZEDONG

• • •

The system of private property is the most important guaranty of freedom, not only for those who own property, but scarcely less for those who do not.
—FRIEDRICH AUGUST VON HAYEK

• • •

At its core, belief in capitalism is belief in mankind.
—JOHAN NORBERG, *In Defense of Global Capitalism* (2003)

• • •

Capitalism has always been a failure for the lower classes. It is now beginning to fail for the middle classes.
—HOWARD ZINN, *A People's History of the United States* (1995)

• • •

It is just as illogical to suggest abolishing capitalism because it hasn't abolished poverty as it would be to suggest abolishing the churches because the churches haven't abolished sin.
—C. DONALD DALLAS, *The Forbes Book of Business Quotations* (1997)

• • •

[T]oday we also have to say "thou shalt not" to an economy of exclusion and inequality…masses of people find themselves excluded and marginalized.
—POPE FRANCIS

• • •

Trickle-Down Economics

There are two ideas of government. There are those who believe that if you just legislate to make the well-to-do prosperous, that their prosperity will leak through on those below. The Democratic idea has been that if you legislate to make the masses prosperous their prosperity will find its way up and through every class that rests upon it.
—WILLIAM JENNINGS BRYAN

• • •

[W]hat an older and less elegant generation called the horse-and-sparrow theory: If you feed the horse enough oats, some will pass through to the road for the sparrows.
—JOHN KENNETH GALBRAITH

• • •

[S]ome people continue to defend trickle-down theories, which assume that economic growth, encouraged by a free market, will inevitably succeed in bringing about greater justice and inclusiveness in the world. This opinion, which has never been confirmed by the facts, expresses a crude and naïve trust in the goodness of those wielding economic power and in the sacralized workings of the prevailing economic system. Meanwhile, the excluded are still waiting.

—POPE FRANCIS

• • •

The Stock Market and Wall Street

The United States has a new weapon. It destroys people, but leaves buildings still standing. It's called the stock market.
—JAY LENO

• • •

Markets can remain irrational longer than you can remain solvent.
—JOHN MAYNARD KEYNES

• • •

WALL STREET, n. A symbol for sin for every devil to rebuke. That Wall Street is a den of thieves is a belief that serves every successful thief in place of a hope in Heaven.
—AMBROSE BIERCE, *The Devil's Dictionary* (1911)

• • •

One of the funny things about the stock market is that every time one person buys, another sells, and both think they are astute.
—WILLIAM FEATHER

• • •

The greater fool theory (GFT) refers to those who buy an investment based on the premise they will be able to sell it at a profit to a "greater fool." Many investors subscribe to this theory, but don't know they are engaging in it. In an ironic twist, they become the "greater fool."
—DANIEL R. SOLIN

Socialism

[S]ocialism is more a matter of equal redistribution of wealth and creation of a welfare state. In order for a welfare state to be created, taxes must be higher so the government can cover its expenses.
—MARKO CEPERKOVIC

• • •

The problem with socialism is that you eventually run out of other people's money.
—MARGARET THATCHER (attributed)

• • •

Socialism only works in two places: Heaven, where they don't need it, and Hell, where they already have it.
— RONALD REAGAN

• • •

Socialism in general has a record of failure so blatant that only an intellectual could ignore or evade it.
—THOMAS SOWELL

• • •

As with the Christian religion, the worst advertisement for Socialism is its adherents.
—GEORGE ORWELL, *The Road to Wigan Pier* (1937)

• • •

Socialism had its sixty years, and it failed miserably.
—EUGENE FAMA

• • •

Communism

In this sense, the theory of the Communists may be summed up in the single sentence: Abolition of private property.
—KARL MARX and FRIEDRICH ENGELS, *The Communist Manifesto* (1848)

• • •

A specter is haunting Europe—the specter of Communism. All the powers of old Europe have entered in a holy alliance to exorcise this specter: Pope and Czar, Meternich and Guizot, French Radicals and German police spies.
—KARL MARX and FRIEDRICH ENGELS, *The Communist Manifesto* (1848)

• • •

If Karl, instead of writing a lot about capital, had made a lot of it, it would have been much better.
—KARL MARX'S MOTHER, HENRIETTA (attributed)

• • •

Capitalism, it is said, is a system wherein man exploits man.
And communism—is vice versa.
—DANIEL BELL

• • •

The principal lesson Soviet economic planning has to teach us
is how it should not be done.
—TAYAR ZAVALANI

• • •

The National Debt, a.k.a. The Federal Debt

There are two ways to conquer and enslave a country. One is by the sword. The other is by debt.
—JOHN ADAMS

• • •

A national debt, if it is not excessive, will be to us a national blessing.
—ALEXANDER HAMILTON

• • •

I go on the principle that a public debt is a public curse, and in a Republican Government a greater curse than any other.
—JAMES MADISON

• • •

We don't have a trillion-dollar debt because we haven't taxed
enough; we have a trillion-dollar debt because
we spend too much.
—RONALD REAGAN

• • •

I found this national debt, doubled, wrapped in a big bow
waiting for me as I stepped into the Oval Office.
—BARACK OBAMA

• • •

Mr. Obama denounced the $2.3 trillion added to the national
debt on Mr. Bush's watch as "deficits as far as the eye can see."
But Mr. Obama's budget adds $9.3 trillion to the debt over the
next ten years. What happened to Obama the deficit hawk?
—KARL ROVE

• • •

The United States has a history of unusual concern about federal (although not state) budget deficits, going back to the earliest days after adoption of the Constitution…deficits are a deeply rooted symbol in American history, the meaning of which has changed over time, but that continually relates to distrust of the national government.

—DANIEL SHAVIRO, *Do Deficits Matter?* (1997)

• • •

No pecuniary consideration is more urgent than the regular redemption and discharge of the public debt; on none can delay be more injurious, or an economy of time more valuable.

—GEORGE WASHINGTON

• • •

The consequences arising from the continual accumulation of public debts in other countries ought to admonish us to be careful to prevent their growth in our own. The national defense must be provided for as well as the support of Government; but both should be accomplished as much as possible by immediate taxes, and as little as possible by loans.

—JOHN ADAMS

• • •

We the People

insure domestic Tranquility, provide for the common defence
and our Posterity, do ordain and establish this Constitution

Article

Section. 1. All legislative Powers herein granted shall be
Representatives.

Section. 2. The House of Representatives shall be composed
shall have the Qualifications requisite for Electors of the
shall be a Representative who shall not have a
when elected, be an Inhabitant of that State in wh
and direct Taxes shall be apportioned among
by adding to the whole Number of
Persons. The actual Enumeration
of ten Years, in such Manner as
have at Least one Representative
Rhode Island and Pro
North Carolina
from any
their Speaker and o
shall be composed of tw

The Senate
Senator shall have one Vote.
Immediately after they sh
Class at
Legislature of any
such Vacancies.

No Person shall be a Senator
not, when elected, be an Inhabitant of that Sta
The Vice President of the United States
The Senate shall chuse their other Officers
President of the United States.

The Senate shall have the sole Power to try all Impeachments
the United States, the Chief Justice shall preside: And no Person shall
Judgment in Cases of Impeachment shall
or Profit under the United States
according to

Chapter 10

The Politics of Human Rights

We hold these Truths to be self-evident, that all Men are created equal, that they are endowed by their Creator with certain unalienable Rights, that among these are Life, Liberty, and the pursuit of Happiness.
—OPENING LINES OF *THE DECLARATION OF INDEPENDENCE*

• • •

The Declaration of Independence ... [is the] declaratory charter of our rights, and of the rights of man.
—THOMAS JEFFERSON

• • •

The Declaration of Independence was not meant for me: that its chief architect, Thomas Jefferson, was a slave owner; that the 13th, 14th, and 15th amendments have not been fully implemented, and the "land of the free" and "sweet land of liberty" are not equally applicable to black and white.
—BENJAMIN MAYS, *Born to Rebel: An Autobiography* (1971)

• • •

The marriage institution cannot exist among slaves, and one-sixth of the population of democratic America is denied its privileges by the law of the land.

What is to be thought of a nation boasting of its liberty, boasting of its humanity, boasting of its Christianity, boasting of its love of justice and purity, and yet having within its own borders three millions of persons denied by law the right of marriage?
—FREDERICK DOUGLASS, *My Bondage and My Freedom* (1855)

• • •

Race

[I] am not, nor ever have been, in favor of bringing about in any way the social and political equality of the white and black races, that I am not, nor ever have been, in favor of making voters or jurors of Negroes, nor of qualifying them to hold office, nor to intermarry with white people... there is a physical difference between the white and black races which I believe will forever forbid the two races living together on terms of social and political equality.... I do not perceive that because the white man is to have the superior position the Negro should be denied everything.
—ABRAHAM LINCOLN

• • •

We have learned to fly the air like birds and swim the sea like fish, but we have not learned the simple art of living together as brothers.
—DR. MARTIN LUTHER KING JR.,
Strength to Love (1963)

• • •

I do not see how a people that can find in its conscience any excuse whatever for slowly burning to death a human being, or for tolerating such an act, can be entrusted with the salvation of a race.
—JAMES WELDON JOHNSON,
Along This Way (1933)

• • •

And little lads, lynchers that were to be,
Danced round the dreadful thing in fiendish glee.
—CLAUDE MCKAY, *The Lynching* (1922)

• • •

Racism is the American form of original sin.
—RALPH ELLISON

• • •

When you're sharing a foxhole with another man, you don't worry about what color he is, just whether or not he will protect your back.
—LEE BENSON

• • •

Slavery

And he that stealeth a man, and selleth him, or if he be found
in his hand, he shall surely be put to death.
—EXODUS 21:16

• • •

True democracy makes no enquiry about the color of skin,
or the place of nativity. Wherever it sees man, it recognizes a
being endowed by his Creator with original inalienable rights.
—SALMON P. CHASE

• • •

The law of the Creator, which invests every human being with
an inalienable title to freedom, cannot be repealed by any
interior law which asserts that man is property.
—SALMON P. CHASE

• • •

They [slaves and their descendants] are not included, and are not intended to be included under the word "citizens" in the Constitution, and can therefore claim none of the rights and privileges which that instrument provides for and secures to citizens of the United States.

—ROGER B. TANEY, majority opinion,
Dred Scott v. Sandford

• • •

One hundred years ago, the slave was freed. One hundred years later, the Negro remains in bondage to the color of his skin. The Negro today asks justice. We do not answer him—we do not answer those who lie beneath this soil—when we reply to the Negro by asking, "Patience."

—LYNDON B. JOHNSON

• • •

Gender

The history of mankind is a history of repeated injuries and usurpations on the part of man toward woman.
—ELIZABETH CADY STANTON

• • •

We ask justice, we ask equality, we ask that all civil and political rights that belong to the citizens of the United States be guaranteed to us and our daughters forever.
—SUSAN B. ANTHONY, ELIZABETH CADY STANTON, MATILDA JOSLYN GAGE, and IDA HUSTED HARPER

• • •

I know nothing of man's rights, or woman's rights; human rights are all that I recognise.
—SARAH GRIMKÉ, *Letters on the Equality of the Sexes and the Condition of Woman* (1838)

• • •

The single most impressive fact about the attempt by
American women to obtain the right to
vote is how long it took.
—ALICE SCHAERR ROSSI

• • •

I am working for the time when unqualified blacks, browns,
and women join the unqualified men in running
our government.
—FRANCES "SISSY" FARENTHOLD

• • •

I think it's about time we voted for senators with breasts. After
all, we've been voting for boobs long enough.
—CLAIRE SARGENT

• • •

Sexuality

If a person is homosexual by nature—that is, if one's sexuality is as intrinsic a part of one's identity as gender or skin color—then society can no more deny a gay person access to the secular rights and religious sacraments because of his homosexuality than it can reinstate Jim Crow.
—JON MEACHAM

• • •

You don't have to be straight to shoot straight.
—BARRY GOLDWATER

• • •

Regarding the moves to repeal the "don't ask, don't tell" policy: I believe that homosexual acts between individuals are immoral, and that we should not condone immoral acts. . . . I do not believe that the armed forces are well served by saying through our policies that it's okay to be immoral in any way, not just with regards to homosexual acts.
—PETER PACE

• • •

Dear Miss Manners: What should I say when I am introduced to a homosexual couple?

Gentle Reader: "How do you do?"

—MISS MANNERS, PEN NAME FOR JUDITH MARTIN, *Miss Manners' Guide to Excruciatingly Correct Behavior* (1982)

• • •

As long as our culture makes coming out an act of civil disobedience, being gay will be a political statement. Accept, at least for now, that your sexuality has political ramifications.

—KENNETH HANES, *The Gay Guy's Guide to Life* (1994)

• • •

My sexuality is my own sexuality. It doesn't belong to anybody. Not to my government, not to my brother, my sister, my family. No.

—ASHRAF ZANATI

• • •

DOMA writes inequality into the entire United States Code. . . . Among the over 1,000 statutes and numerous federal regulations that DOMA controls are laws pertaining to Social Security, housing, taxes, criminal sanctions, copyright, and veterans' benefits.
—ANTHONY KENNEDY

• • •

If the widespread practice of homosexuality will bring about the destruction of your nation, if it will bring about terrorist bombs, if it'll bring about earthquakes, tornadoes and possibly a meteor, it isn't necessarily something we ought to open our arms to.
—PAT ROBERTSON

• • •

I always get the feeling that when lesbians look at me, they're thinking, "That's why I'm not a heterosexual."
—GEORGE COSTANZA, *Seinfeld*

• • •

I say let them marry. Why shouldn't they be as miserable as the rest of us?
—JACK MCCOY, *Law & Order*

• • •

Abortion

I've noticed that everyone that is for abortion
has already been born.
—RONALD REAGAN

• • •

If men could get pregnant, abortion would be a sacrament.
—FLORYNCE KENNEDY

• • •

Every person has the right to have his life respected. This right
shall be protected by law and, in general, from the moment of
conception. No one shall be arbitrarily deprived of his life.
—AMERICAN CONVENTION ON HUMAN
RIGHTS, Article 4

• • •

Supporters of [the Human Life Amendment] are often eloquent in their defense of the fertilized egg but are seldom willing to aid the woman whose body nourishes it.
—CAROLE ANDERSON and LEE CAMPBELL

• • •

The states are not free, under the guise of protecting maternal health or potential life, to intimidate women into continuing pregnancies.
—HARRY BLACKMUN

• • •

Everybody is right when it comes to the issue of abortion.
—ALAN DERSHOWITZ

• • •

For today, the women of this Nation still retain the liberty to control their destinies. But the signs are evident and very ominous, and a chill wind blows.
—HARRY BLACKMUN

• • •

I think the Supreme Court's decision in Roe versus Wade was
wrong and should be overturned.
—GEORGE H. W. BUSH

• • •

One of our fundamental rights is the right to make
independent reproductive decisions.
—FAYE WATTLETON

• • •

Well, as you know, there are many things in life that are not
fair, that wealthy people can afford and poor people can't.
But I don't believe that the Federal Government should take
action to try to make these opportunities exactly equal,
particularly when there is a moral factor involved.
—JIMMY CARTER

• • •

I am opposed to abortion and to government funding of
abortions. We should not spend state funds on abortions
because so many people believe abortion is wrong.
—BILL CLINTON

• • •

Obama: I am pro-choice.

Reporter: In all situations including the late term thing?

Obama: I am pro-choice. I believe that women make responsible choices and they know better than anybody the tragedy of a difficult pregnancy and I don't think that it's the government's role to meddle in that choice.

—BARACK OBAMA

• • •

If babies had guns they wouldn't be aborted.

—SLOGAN, Senatorial primary campaign of Texas GOP congressman Steve Stockman

• • •

If it's a legitimate rape, the female body has ways to try to shut that whole thing down.

—TODD AKIN

• • •

Guns

A well regulated Militia, being necessary to the security of a free State, the right of the people to keep and bear Arms, shall not be infringed.
—SECOND AMENDMENT TO *THE UNITED STATES CONSTITUTION*

• • •

A free people ought...to be armed.
—GEORGE WASHINGTON

• • •

If guns are outlawed, only outlaws will have guns.
—ANONYMOUS

• • •

Forty-seven percent of American adults currently report that they have a gun in their home or elsewhere on their property.
—GALLUP POLL

• • •

[The] National Rifle Association is always arguing that the Second Amendment determines the right to bear arms. But I think it really is the people's right to bear arms in a militia. The NRA thinks it protects their right to have Teflon-coated bullets. But that's not the original understanding.
—ROBERT BORK

• • •

You could say that the paparazzi and the tabloids are sort of the "assault weapons" of the First Amendment. They're ugly, a lot of people don't like them, but they're protected by the First Amendment—just as "assault weapons" are protected by the Second Amendment.
—CHARLTON HESTON

• • •

The right to keep and bear arms is granted by God and protected from government aggression by the Constitution.
—STEVE STOCKMAN

• • •

What people all over the country fear today is being abandoned by their government. If a tornado hits, if a hurricane hits, if a riot occurs, that they're going to be out there alone, and the only way they will protect themselves, in the cold, in the dark, when they are vulnerable, is with a firearm.
—WAYNE LaPIERRE

• • •

I'll give you my gun when you take it from my cold, dead hands.
—NRA BUMPER STICKER

• • •

The answer to crime is not gun control; it is law enforcement and self-control.
—ALAN KEYES

• • •

The gun-buying public is not going away.
—RANDY CLOUD

• • •

After a shooting spree, they always want to take the guns away from the people who didn't do it. I sure as hell wouldn't want to live in a society where the only people allowed guns are the police and the military.
—WILLIAM S. BURROUGHS

• • •

[W]ay too many gun owners still seem to believe that any regulation of the right to keep and bear arms is an infringement [of the Second Amendment]. The fact is, all constitutional rights are regulated, always have been, and need to be.
—DICK METCALF

• • •

Gods, Guns and Guts Made America Great.
—AMERICAN SAYING

Privacy

On average, each day the [US National Security Agency] was able to extract . . . More than 5 million missed-call alerts, for use in contact-chaining analysis (working out someone's social network from who they contact and when).
—JAMES BALL

• • •

Now, the reforms I'm proposing today should give the American people greater confidence that their rights are being protected, even as our intelligence and law enforcement agencies maintain the tools they need to keep us safe.
—BARACK OBAMA

• • •

[T]he whole point of intelligence is to obtain information that is not publicly available. But America's capabilities are unique, and the power of new technologies means that there are fewer and fewer technical constraints on what we can do. That places a special obligation on us to ask tough questions about what we should do.
—BARACK OBAMA

• • •

With its powers of compulsion and criminal prosecution, the government poses unique threats to privacy when it collects data on its own citizens. Government collection of personal information on such a massive scale also courts the ever-present danger of "mission creep." An even more compelling danger is that personal information collected by the government will be misused to harass, blackmail, or intimidate, or to single out for scrutiny particular individuals or groups.
—PRIVACY AND CIVIL LIBERTIES
OVERSIGHT BOARD

• • •

[T]he statute only authorizes the FBI to collect information from the telephone providers, and yet it's the NSA that receives the information.
—PRIVACY AND CIVIL LIBERTIES OVERSIGHT BOARD, from a statement by five of the seven members

• • •

Immigration

A stranger, if just, is not only to be preferred before a
countryman, but a kinsman.
—PYTHAGORAS

• • •

Our country is wherever we are well off.
—CICERO

• • •

The bosom of America is open to receive not only the Opulent
and respectable Stranger, but the oppressed and persecuted
of all Nations And Religions; whom we shall welcome to a
participation of all our rights and privileges, if by decency and
propriety of conduct they appear to merit the enjoyment.
—GEORGE WASHINGTON

• • •

This commingling here of all nationalities under the blessing of God will produce in seventy-five or one hundred years the most magnificent style of man and woman the world ever saw. They will have the wit of one race, the eloquence of another race, the kindness of another, the generosity of another, the aesthetic taste of another, the high moral character of another, and when that man and woman step forth, their brain and nerve and muscle an intertwining of the fibres of all nationalities . . .
—THOMAS DE WITT TALMAGE

• • •

Born in iniquity and conceived in sin, the spirit of *nationalism* has never ceased to bend human institutions to the service of dissension and distress.
—THORSTEIN VEBLEN

• • •

Let us say to the immigrant not that we hope he will learn English, but that he has got to learn it. Let the immigrant who does not learn it go back. He has got to consider the interest of the United States or he should not stay here.
—THEODORE ROOSEVELT

• • •

Remember, remember always, that all of us, and you and I especially, are descended from immigrants and revolutionists.
—FRANKLIN D. ROOSEVELT

• • •

In no other realm of our national life are we so hampered and stultified by the dead hand of the past, as we are in this field of immigration.
—HARRY S. TRUMAN

• • •

Today, as never before, untold millions are storming our gates for admission and those gates are cracking under the strain. The solution of the problems of Europe and Asia will not come through a transplanting of those problems en masse to the United States.
—PAT McCARRAN

• • •

A nation that cannot control its borders is not a nation.
—RONALD REAGAN

• • •

We've doubled the funding for border security since I took
office. We now spend $10 billion a year to protect this border.
—GEORGE W. BUSH

• • •

Some of the hardest-working and most productive people in
this city are undocumented aliens.
—RUDOLPH GIULIANI

• • •

More than any other nation on Earth, America has
constantly drawn strength and spirit from wave after wave of
immigrants. In each generation they have proved to be the
most restless, the most adventurous, the most innovative, the
most industrious of people.
—BILL CLINTON

• • •

I fear that in the next century we will have many more
Muslims in the United States if we do not adopt the strict
immigration policies that I believe are necessary to preserve
the values and beliefs traditional to the United States of
America and to prevent our resources from being swamped.
—VIRGIL GOODE

• • •

We can't go on with this broken system, because if we are
here another five years from now and we haven't fixed it, there
will be even more people here illegally.

—KELLY AYOTTE

• • •

We're running an H.M.O. for illegal immigrants and if we
keep it up, we're going to bankrupt the county.

—MICHAEL D. ANTONOVICH

• • •

A mass legalization, or amnesty, of millions of illegal aliens,
combined with an increase in future immigration, will have
profound consequences for every law enforcement officer
in the country and especially those who enforce our nation's
immigration laws.

—CHRIS CRANE

• • •

Immigration reform is important to expanding opportunity
as well. Why? Because throughout our history immigrants
have brought innovation, ideas, investment, and dynamism to
American enterprise.

—THOMAS J. DONOHUE

• • •

Until we revolutionized legal immigration services they had
not changed since Abraham Lincoln practiced law.
—TWEET VISANOW @VISANOW

• • •

This isn't the first time that there's been some ugliness around
the issue of immigration.
—LINDSEY GRAHAM

• • •

Immigration is the sincerest form of flattery.
—JACK PAAR

• • •

Index

Index

Index